Dog Stars

Astrology for Dog Lovers

VIKING STUDIO

VIKING STUDIO
Published by the Penguin Group
Penguin Group (USA) Inc., 375 Hudson Street, New York, New York 10014, U.S.A. • Penguin Group (Canada), 90 Eglinton Avenue East, Suite 700, Toronto, Ontario, Canada M4P 2Y3 (a division of Pearson Penguin Canada Inc.) • Penguin Books Ltd, 80 Strand, London WC2R 0RL, England • Penguin Ireland, 25 St. Stephen's Green, Dublin 2, Ireland (a division of Penguin Books Ltd) • Penguin Books Australia Ltd, 250 Camberwell Road, Camberwell, Victoria 3124, Australia (a division of Pearson Australia Group Pty Ltd) • Penguin Books India Pvt Ltd, 11 Community Centre, Panchsheel Park, New Delhi – 110 017, India • Penguin Group (NZ), Cnr Airborne and Rosedale Roads, Albany, Auckland 1310, New Zealand (a division of Pearson New Zealand Ltd) • Penguin Books (South Africa) (Pty) Ltd, 24 Sturdee Avenue, Rosebank, Johannesburg 2196, South Africa

Penguin Books Ltd, Registered Offices: 80 Strand, London WC2R 0RL, England

First published in 2006 by Viking Studio, a member of Penguin Group (USA) Inc.

10 9 8 7 6 5 4 3 2 1

PHOTOGRAPHS BY WENDY LAM

ISBN 0-14-200513-4

Printed in the United States of America

Designed by Katy Riegel

This book is dedicated to

Blossom and Roxanna Maria Schostak (Roxy) and Clive

—Sherene

This book is dedicated to

my favorite weimies, Monkey and Franz

—Wendy

Acknowledgments

Love and Gratitude:
Mom and Dad
Tara and Jen at RLR for all their hard work
and support with this book.
Wendy.

All Friends and Fam:
Mom and Dad, Kerry, Dom, Tet, Gad, Nil, Rachel, Todd, Anne, Natasha,
Stefanie, Neena and Zack, all grandmas, grandpas, aunts, uncles,
cousins, ancestors, etc.

Special thanks to:
RLR—Tara and Jennifer Unter
Ammachi for blessing the world.
Bill Maher for being my comic inspiration.

Acknowledgments

All clients past and present.
The Collective.
Sant Ambroeus family.
All doggies everywhere—may they continue to teach
the rest of us dummies about unconditional love.

Lokah Samastah Sukinoh Bhavantu.
—Sherene

The Canines I would like to give special thanks to:
Lisa for teaching me about puppy love.
Bruno for teaching me about loyalty.
Rocky for teaching me about devotion.
Tiger for teaching me about courage.
Monkey for teaching me about happiness.
Blossom for teaching me about ZaZen.
Cora for teaching me about fairness.
Roxy for teaching me about sweetness.
Jhu Jhai for teaching my parents how to enjoy life to the fullest again.
Franz for teaching me and your dada about maximum
true unconditional love and the secrets to
staying young and blissful.
Our super *Dog Stars* models for teaching me how
to have the best time at work.

The humans I would like to give special thanks to:
Mom for introducing me to my first best friend.
Dad for your generosity and endless love and support.

Acknowledgments

Anita and Gerd Till for giving us the best gift in the world—Franz.
Victor and Wilbur for always being real.
Grandma, Helen and Sophie, and all my aunties, uncles and cousins.
Jo Jo, Phyllis, Quy, Alisa, Kerry, Lizzie, Peter, Jen, Ian, Dominique,
Christine, Swati, Tracey, Rachel, Lisa, Margaret, Nathan, Edmond,
Paul, Amos, and Nadia for their genuine friendship.
Verena for being my best dork-out buddy, sunshine, and assistant.
Franzi's amazing dada, Joachim, for his unconditional love,
endless support, and assistance.
Dog Stars wouldn't have come to life without him.

The beautiful souls at the Door for always keeping my spirits up.
My photo editor, Yun Li.
The proud owners of all the Super *Dog Stars* models.
My co-author, Sherene.
Our literary agents, Tara and Jen, for all their help and support.
Publisher, Megan Newman, Editor, Dara Stewart, Associate Editor, Meg Leder,
Assistant Editor, Rebecca Behan, and the staff at Penguin Group
for giving us this brilliant opportunity.

Peace and Love,
Wendy

Thank you, Park Slope Books and Sant Ambroeus, for sharing your locations.

Contents

Contents

Introduction

WHETHER YOU'RE NEWLY in the market for a beloved soul mate or you're already in a committed relationship, you're holding in your hands the ultimate guide to developing a star-struck match with the most important creature in your life: your dog!

Using time-tested astrology principles, *Dog Stars* is here to guide you on the cosmic path to finding the perfect dog and human relationship. You'll learn what different pooches look for in owners, and why some dogs slobber you with kisses while others can't be bothered. You'll discover what breeds are best for your astrological sign, as well as what star sign your dog embodies. You'll gain insight into your pooch's psyche: If your dog could talk, just what would he or she want to tell you?

Whether you're looking to get a dog, or are hoping to improve your current relationship with your pet, this book will help to match you up with a breed that suits your own sign personality and will help you better understand your pet. Just as human-to-human star-sign compatibility is important in assessing the pros and cons of relating to each other, so too is dog and human star-sign compatibility helpful in understanding and strengthening the harmony between you and your dog. For example, a typical Sagittarian dog breed would be the free-spirited and adventurous German shorthaired pointer. And what dog better embodies the traits of the fiery and bouncy Aries than the sassy dachshund? Based on the dog breeds' typical signs, you can then figure how to best interact with each sign, and which breed best fits your own sign's personality. For example, what does a stubborn, determined Taurus dog look for in an owner as opposed to a homebound Cancer pooch? If you're a pragmatic Capricorn human, which canine would suit you best: the affable Aquarius or the flashy Leo dog star? Of course, there are no absolutes when it comes to the fine art of dog-human matchmaking, but our specially designed *Dog Star* Compatibility Guide can have a tremendous impact on the quality of daily relations. *Dog Stars* will only further enhance and glorify the sacred bond between the two of you.

Although dogs certainly have their fair share of typical behaviors in common, such as eating, sleeping, and barking, no two dogs are exactly alike. The more you know about the tiniest details of what makes your bundle of joy tick, the better equipped you will be in training, loving, and serving your soul mate. *Dog Stars* is designed to inform and entertain you with illustrations of typical personality traits normally assigned to humans but modified into doggie terminology. Just because dogs don't speak using words does not mean that they are any less complex or evolved than human beings (some may even argue they're more evolved!). It is just as essential for owners to understand the inner workings of the canine psyche, and *Dog Stars* unlocks the key to truly understanding the temperaments, habits, personality traits, and preferences of your pooch. In the end, you'll discover a newfound appreciation for the many lovable nuances of your best friend!

WHY ASTROLOGY WORKS AND
WHY IT WORKS FOR YOUR DOG

Because we say so. No, but seriously . . . you can scoff at the lack of scientific evidence if you must; but who doesn't at least glance at their horoscope in the newspapers and in magazines whenever they get a chance? Of course if that's been your only exposure to the deep and fascinating realm of astrology so far, you may think astrology is complete nonsense or exists for sheer entertainment value only. Well, the proof of the pudding is in the eating: Match the traits of the *zodiac* sign to the person (or dog!) and tell us if they don't match up. Of course there are always exceptions to any and every rule, but we believe you'll find that the semblance between *zodiac* sign and personality is more obvious than you might think. For example, it would be hard to confuse a spastic and exuberant Sagittarius dog with a sleepy and dreamy Pisces pooch.

Dogs are not so dissimilar from humans in that they exhibit many of the same basic human expressions and emotions such as happiness, confusion, excitement, impatience, sadness, loneliness, and longing. They even worry about what happened to you when you come home later than expected. It makes sense that the ancient system of astrology as a powerful symbolic system and language would also apply to the equally complex guardians of the human race. Most of the sym-

✳

bols of Astrology are based on animals anyway, so chances are astrology, being part of nature, really speaks to the inner animal in all of us. Dogs are just as influenced, if not more so, by the celestial bodies as humans. For proof, just watch their behavior around a full moon—they'll be more restless and hyper—perhaps chasing after their tails for no reason.

If you're one of those right-brained types, consider the fact that water accounts for more than two-thirds of the mass of the human body. Certainly science has proven that the moon causes the tides of the earth's oceans. Could we not surmise then, that the planetary bodies have some kind of gravitational pull on humans as well? And our friends on four legs are even more in tune with nature and the heavenly bodies, so this should hold doubly true for dog stars. Why not have a little fun with this and see for yourself?

Astrology is a wonderful tool for humans to not only gain a deeper understanding of themselves, but more important, to really uncover the mystery of why Spot has certain idiosyncrasies that just can't otherwise be explained. To get started, all you need to know is the date that Spot came into the world. So if you're buying a dog, be sure to ask the breeder or the pet shop for all the stats on your pup. If you don't know your dog's birth date, you can use the *It's in the Stars* chart on page xxii for an on-the-spot analysis of his personality as it relates to his breed. You can also take the fun little *What's My Sign? Quiz* on pages xxiv to xxx to figure out his sign. For more on determining your dog's sign, see *"Hey, Doggie, What's Your Sign?"* on pages xx to xxii.

HEY, BABY, WHAT'S YOUR SIGN?

Unfortunately, everyone's heard this pathetic pickup line before! The answer you'd give to that question is what astrologers call the Sun sign, also known in lay circles as one's star sign. Technically speaking, this is the constellation or zodiac sign the sun occupied on the day you were born. The same goes for your pooch. However, in order to stamp out any confusion and for the sake of consistency with our book's title, *Dog Stars,* we instead decided to refer to the "Sun sign" as the "star sign."

Star signs are broken down into the four elements: earth, air, fire, and water. The fire signs—Aries, Leo, and Sagittarius—are the feisty, go-getter signs of the zodiac. They like to get the party started and keep everyone enthused with their dynamic energy. Fire burns through things quickly and likes to create warmth wherever it travels. It's the same with the fire sign doggies: You instantly feel their energy, warmth, and exuberance.

In contrast, the water signs—Cancer, Scorpio, and Pisces—are more sensitive and easily influenced by the feelings and moods of those around them. Like water, they are more impressionable and changeable depending on their environment. They are intuitive and full of depth.

Air signs—Gemini, Libra, and Aquarius—are the movers and shakers of the zodiac, flitting from one social encounter to the next—they're forever curious. Dogs under these signs surely wish they could speak because they have a lot to say.

Finally, the earth signs—Taurus, Virgo, and Capricorn—of the zodiac hold it all together. They are the glue, the solid ground, and the most reliable of all the elements. They tend to be more cautious and plodding than the other elements.

✳

Star signs are also broken down into what in astrology are called modalities. The "modes"—or "M.O.'s," as they may be more commonly referred to in lay lingo—are the ways the different signs tend to operate. For instance, fixed signs—Taurus, Leo, Scorpio, and Aquarius—are the modes that stay the course no matter what; they are the most stubborn and loyal of all the modes. Mutable signs—Gemini, Virgo, Sagittarius, Pisces—are the most malleable and adaptable of all the signs; they mutate according to the situation or people they are with. Cardinal signs—Aries, Cancer, Libra, Capricorn—are the initiators and the social signs of the zodiac. They are connected with the four cardinal points—Spring, Summer, Fall, Winter—which mark the seasons, and thus are linked with initiating new beginnings.

RULERSHIPS

Each sign of the zodiac is assigned at least one planetary ruler. Some signs like Scorpio, Aquarius, and Pisces have more than one ruler. They at one time had to share their ruling planets with other signs until more planets were discovered and each was given its own ruler. For example, Scorpio used to share Mars as the ruler along with Aries until Pluto was discovered, which seemed to better represent Scorpio's dark, mysterious underworld qualities. When zany Uranus was discovered, it seemed fitting to assign that planet to Aquarius, which formerly had to share the rulership of Saturn with Capricorn. Similarly, Pisces used to share the rulership of Jupiter with Sagittarius until Neptune was discovered, which seemed to fit better with the vague, murky characteristics of Pisces. As you may have already guessed, rulerships of planets to zodiac signs are based on a natural affinity between the two. Mars as the red planet seems fitting to govern the fiery, red-hot-tempered Aries, while it makes sense that the goddess of beauty, Venus, would rule both temperate Taurus and lovely Libra. You'll find the guide for the rulers at the beginning of each Dog Star chapter.

GETTING STARTED

In the following pages, you'll find all the guidance and information you need to create a heavenly relationship with your dog. Chapters are broken down by star signs; each begins with the list of typical breeds for the respective sign, and you will find out what each sign's element, modality, and rulership is. Then we will give you the ins and outs of each sign's personality traits and characteristics and help you figure out exactly what kind of pooch you are dealing with.

After you have all that information under your belt, you'll learn how to listen to your pooch. Based on a dog's star sign characteristics and our having spent our lives paying very close attention to our friends in Dogdom, we feel extremely privileged to be able to translate what the doggies would like to say to their human companions. For example, the Leo doggie says, "I'm the bomb!"

If you are starting your search for a pal or just trying to improve the current relationship with your doggie partner, the following section gives you all the secrets of what the pooch of each sign looks for in his/her human companion, straight from the doggie's perspective. For example, a Virgo pooch would say,

✳

"I am looking for someone who appreciates a Zen-like minimalism in his or her surroundings, or a classic elegance in the home environment." We'll also give you a bonus list on how to earn brownie points from your pooch so you can please him/her to the max.

Next, you will learn about how each dog's star sign matches up with the human's star sign; in other words, are you compatible with your doggie or not? Does a Libra human get along with a Leo pooch? Is it love at first sight? Or do you need to work on your relationship?

The last part of each chapter features the real-life case examples and stories of every star sign's featured models. They are all natural beauties. Their beauty tips: true love and happiness.

HEY, DOGGIE, WHAT'S YOUR SIGN?

Now that you know the basics, let's go on to the next step: identifying your dog's star sign!

IF YOU KNOW YOUR DOG'S BIRTHDAY

Look up your dog's star sign in the table of contents or in the *It's in the Stars* chart on pages xxii to xxiv and go to the chapter corresponding to your dog's sign. There you'll find everything you need to know about your dog's star sign characteristics and personality traits plus training tidbits and much more. Then study the compatibility guide to see if you are a good match. For example, if your pooch is a Pisces and you're a Taurus, are you the perfect couple or will you need some advice from obedience school?

IF YOU DON'T KNOW YOUR DOG'S BIRTHDAY

Not to worry! We've matched up typical breeds that suit each star sign personality. Simply look for a beautiful close-up shot of your doggie's breed and you will find the chapter you want. If you don't see a photo of your pooch's breed, go to the *It's in the Stars* chart following this section and look up your dog's breed to see what sign he/she is. Then go to the chapter for that sign and study all you need to know about your pooch. For example, a golden retriever is a typical Libra, born to please and charm and please some more. . . .

IF YOU'RE IN THE MARKET FOR A POOCH

This handy guide allows you to research your compatibility with any potential partner in crime, helping you see which breed suits you best. Again, you can use the *It's in the Stars* chart to look up a breed you've been eyeing, then study the compatibility guide and see if you would be a good match. For example, if you have been dreaming about getting a pug, you will find that breed in the Pisces chapter. Look for the compatibility guide for your combo and see if you two are a match made in heaven.

WHAT ABOUT MUTTS?

Don't worry! We have a whole chapter dedicated to our popular friends. Those of you who don't know your doggie's specific mixes or birth date can go straight to the Gemini chapter to find a fun and exciting companion who will always keep you guessing like the lovable twins. One minute, the bulldog side of her may want to lie down and chill next to you at a café; the next minute, the spastic German shorthaired pointer side might act up and start chasing after a roller skater carrying a volleyball.

IT'S IN THE STARS: WHAT SIGN IS YOUR BREED?

Use this chart to figure out what sign your
pooch is by birth date or typical breed.

STAR SIGN	TYPICAL BREED
Aries (March 21–April 19)	Dachshund*
	Chihuahua
	Jack Russell Terrier
Taurus (April 20–May 20)	Bulldog*
	Bassett Hound
	French Bulldog
	Saint Bernard
Gemini (May 21–June 20)	Mutt*
Cancer (June 21–July 22)	Great Dane*
	Cavalier King Charles Spaniel
	Scottish Terrier

Leo (July 23–August 22)	Shih Tzu*
	Bichon Frise
	Pekingese
Virgo (August 23–September 22)	Weimaraner*
	Dalmatian
	Hungarian Vizsla
Libra (September 23–October 22)	Labrador Retriever*
	Golden Retriever
	Poodle
Scorpio (October 23–November 21)	German Shepherd*
	Doberman Pinscher
	Rhodesian Ridgeback
Sagittarius (November 22–December 21)	German Shorthaired Pointer*
	Boxer
	Brittany Spaniel
Capricorn (December 22–January 19)	Yorkshire Terrier*
	Bernese Mountain Dog
	Schnauzer
	Shetland Sheepdog

Aquarius (January 20–February 18)	Cocker Spaniel*
	Beagle
	Siberian Husky
Pisces (February 19–March 20)	Pug*
	Collie
	Newfoundland

*Star sightings

WHAT'S MY SIGN? QUIZ

If your pooch's breed is not listed above, no problem! Here's a quiz you can take to figure out what he/she is. Simply mark 1 next to each personality trait and add up the points. The star sign that has the most points is the one for your dog! If 2 or more signs tie, you got it . . . it's probably a Gemini!

ARIES DOG

___Feisty
___Independent
___Self-absorbed
___Yappy
___Pushy
___Aggressive
___Loud
___Accident prone
___Innocent
___Competitive

___Vain
___Impatient
___Courageous
___Heroic
___Fierce
___Bossy
___Fearless
___Energetic
___Resilient
___Pioneering spirit

TOTAL _____ POINTS

TAURUS DOG

___Stubborn
___Determined
___Lazy
___Indulgent
___Hearty appetite
___Devoted
___Reliable
___Relaxed
___Patient
___Loyal

___Possessive
___Slow paced
___Cautious
___Habitual
___Predictable
___Tenacious
___Grounded
___Affectionate
___Soothing
___Good listener

TOTAL _____ POINTS

GEMINI DOG

___Versatile
___Chatty
___Social
___Curious
___Confused
___Smart
___Playful
___Childlike
___Dual personality
___Unpredictable

___Spacey
___Nervous
___High energy
___Loves to travel
___Great student
___Thinker
___Irresponsible
___Trickster
___Silly
___Trendsetter

TOTAL _____ POINTS

CANCER DOG

___Moody
___Sensitive
___Homebound
___Mothering
___Sentimental
___Whiney
___Crabby
___Intuitive/psychic
___Caring
___Thoughtful

___Clingy
___Great memory
___Emotional
___Private
___Antisocial
___Touchy
___Attached
___Exclusive
___Needy
___Loving

TOTAL _____ POINTS

LEO DOG

___Proud
___Glamorous
___Leader
___Dramatic
___Arrogant
___Generous
___Affectionate
___Divaish
___Entitled
___Extra loyal

___Crowd pleaser
___Center of attention
___Regal
___Strong
___Confident
___Courageous
___Dignified
___Spoiled
___Heart of gold
___Performer

TOTAL _____ POINTS

VIRGO DOG

___Picky
___Looks clean
___Neat
___Considerate
___Smart
___Nervous
___Self-conscious
___Hypochondriac
___Repetitive behavior(s)
___Fussy

___Critical
___Health conscious
___Perfectionist
___Likes to serve you
___Loves solitude
___Noise sensitive
___Worries
___Mature at any age
___Fears chaos
___Needs order

TOTAL _____ POINTS

LIBRA DOG

___Moderate
___Pretty
___Fair
___Diplomatic
___Harmonious
___Lazy
___LOVES food
___Sociable
___Agreeable
___Easygoing

___Pleaser
___Charming
___Flirtatious
___Graceful
___Peaceful
___Sweet
___Lighthearted
___Fun
___Indecisive
___Passive

TOTAL _____ POINTS

SCORPIO DOG

___Intense
___Brooding
___Controlling
___Passionate
___Extremist
___Secretive
___Suspicious
___Mysterious
___Demanding
___Jealous

___Intelligent
___Penetrating
___Resourceful
___Sly
___Devoted
___Protective
___Overly sensitive
___Vengeful
___All or nothing
___Psychic

TOTAL _____ POINTS

SAGITTARIUS DOG

___Happy-go-lucky
___Goofy
___Spastic.
___Adventurous
___Optimistic
___Fun loving
___Wild
___Philosophical
___Outdoorsy
___Loves fast cars

___Loud barking
___Expansive
___Clumsy
___Exuberant
___Tireless
___Loves life
___Inspiring
___Extra friendly
___Free spirit
___Fast runner

TOTAL _____ POINTS

CAPRICORN DOG

___Serious
___Irritable
___Wise
___Ambitious
___Status conscious
___Practical
___Simple
___Disciplined
___Self-possessed
___Diligent

___Masterful
___Funny
___Hardheaded
___Traditional
___Dignified
___Industrious
___Mature
___Commands respect
___Classic
___Aloof

TOTAL _____ POINTS

AQUARIUS DOG

___Friendly
___Eccentric
___Quirky
___Experimental
___Genius
___Detached
___Loves groups
___Popular
___Open-minded
___Party animal

___Inventive
___Unpredictable
___Bizarre
___Rebellious
___Anxious
___Restless
___Spontaneous
___Hippielike tendencies
___Chill
___Ahead of the trend

TOTAL _____ POINTS

PISCES DOG

___Sleepaholic
___Dreamy
___Sensitive
___Otherworldly
___Spiritual
___Invisible
___Chameleonlike
___Wishy-washy
___Introverted
___Plays the victim
___Avoidant

___Addictive tendencies
___Compassionate
___Chaotic
___Messy
___Unconditional love
  (especially so)
___Empathic
___Confused
___Tired
___Weak

TOTAL _____ POINTS

MY DOG IS A/AN _____!

ANY QUESTIONS?

Now that you've had a little introduction to the mesmerizing world of canine astrology, you'll no doubt have some well-informed questions. Let us try to anticipate and address such quandaries in advance. . . .

DON'T ALL DOGS BASICALLY HAVE THE SAME PERSONALITIES?

While it is true that most dogs tend to display the wonderful loyal and unconditionally loving traits that so attract us to this animal species in the first place, if you take the time to look a little more closely at your pet's unique personality quirks, you'll surely notice that there are some distinguishing features that make up their endearing personalities. Even the owner of multiple dogs of the same breed will attest to the fact that they each have their own unique personalities.

WHAT IF MY DOG REALLY FITS MORE THAN ONE STAR SIGN PROFILE?

That's okay! Just like with humans, doggies may have their subtle complexities and contradictions. And just as in any personality profiling system there are sure to be overlaps. Our advice is to just use your best judgment and intuition to feel out which of the signs truly captures your doggie's personality best. Chances are if you let go of the doubting mind, the truth will reveal itself to you and you'll see your pup is indeed more one sign than another. And most important, remember this is meant to be fun and useful more than anything. No system is without its glitches, so just enjoy and use whatever information you find the most fun and helpful.

✳

WHAT IF MY DOG STAR AND I AREN'T COMPATIBLE ACCORDING TO THE STAR SIGN COMPATIBILITY GUIDE?

Don't panic! If you knew how many successful and long-lasting marriages were comprised of incompatible star signs, you'd know there is nothing to worry about. We usually attract people and dogs into our life that challenge our worldview and help us grow through the seemingly incompatible differences. No matter what your signs are, you and your dog can learn a lot from each other, and a few bumps in the road are what make life and relationships more interesting.

Dog Stars

DOG STAR

Aries

(March 21–April 19)

THE ARIES DOG

ELEMENT: Fire

MODALITY: Cardinal

RULERSHIP: Mars

SYMBOL: Ram

MOST COMPATIBLE WITH: Gemini, Leo, Sagittarius, and Aquarius

WHAT AN ARIES DOG DAYDREAMS ABOUT: chasing cars; beating up other dogs twice their size; being your hero

KEYWORDS: feisty, aggressive, independent, takes the initiative, rowdy, impulsive, fierce, high-energy, accident-prone

THE ARIES DOG STAR'S PERSONALITY

♈ The Aries dog wants to be the first dog to do everything.

♈ The Aries dog is both macho and heroic.

♈ The Aries dog hates to be kept waiting.

♈ The Aries dog wants it his way, right away.

♈ The Aries dog has a lot of chutzpah.

♈ The Aries dog jumps in face first.

STAR SIGN CHARACTERISTICS

BARK IT LIKE IT'S HOT

Like a furry commando on four legs, an Aries dog will dominate, even if he's small. Nothing and no one can intimidate him. A Mars-ruled pup loves to start fights with all the other dog stars: It makes him feel most alive and reminds him how fierce he is. Patience might be a virtue, but the Aries pooch can live without it: let the Taurus doggies have that one. An Aries dog wants instant gratification, treats, and rewards—yesterday! His pet peeve is being made to wait. When he wants to go out, he means *now,* so bust a move or he'll punish the daylights out of you by ruining your carpet or brand-new Manolos. If you're looking for the Power Off switch, good luck: The Aries dog doesn't have one. Trust that you've found yourself an Energizer bunny–variety dog. You must supply copious amounts of activity or he'll take all his pent-up aggression out on you, your furniture, or on other doggies.

PUT UP YOUR DUKES, DOG!

Watch how your feisty pup just can't resist picking fights with pooches ten times his size; he has to prove his own invincibility. Truth is, the Aries dog is a lovable little hothead with all bark and no bite. He's actually just a noisy little bundle of love dying for you to like him. An Aries dog wants to be your hero. He wants to be the first to do and see everything. He wants to impress you by ramming away the annoying competition and forcing his way up to his rightful place: number one, now and forever.

BARK LOUDLY AND CARRY A BIG STICK

The Aries dog knows how to use and abuse his woof power—quiet time is *so* not his thing. Always on the go, even if it's just chasing his own tail, this restless fur-ball loves to sniff out the next challenge or competition to prove his status (numero uno or bust!). Size and stature is no issue for a warrior dog. Even the smallest amongst the Aries clan would never let size intimidate him. Fiercely defending his honor, he'll step right up to any cocky canine that dares him to a little sidewalk skirmish.

MACHO, MACHO DOG

If you already own an Aries, you can probably guess that subtlety is not your dog's strong suit. When he's happy, you know it, as he pounces all over you and covers you with licks. If he's had it with your human foibles, get ready to feel the wrath—an out-and-out doggie tantrum replete with growls and paw slamming. The goal is to be champ and ruler of the household, neighborhood, and dog run. Have mercy on the wuss of a dog that is clueless enough to step up in this macho dog's face;

they're going down. You may wonder who is master and who is servant in this relationship. Unless you can hold your own, expect a major role reversal unless you love watching your Rambo pooch pitch a fit every time he doesn't get his way.

My Way or the Highway

The Aries dog doesn't like to share, play fair, or put up with other dogs, if he can help it. Fighting to be number one twenty-four hours a day, this fearless fighter will plow his way to the front of the line and still get away with it because underneath all that bravado, he's still just an innocent little pup. But pity the fool who keeps him waiting. He's in a serious rush to get to the next hot spot, and be first doing it.

While he loves to be the boss, the Aries' impulsiveness needs to be kept in check: He's constantly bumping into furniture or sniffing scary things, or even recklessly thinking he can take on oncoming traffic. Be sure to have plenty of soft-edged, child-proof furniture around your home. Discipline and plenty of exercise is the key for tempering this jazzed-up pooch. Teach your Aries puppy how to share and play nice with other doggies early on in life and you'll have fewer battles of the doggie will later on. Wear him out any chance you get so you can sit back and enjoy the innocent and now-mellow Ram-dog energy. Once exhausted, this bundle of energy is a joy to behold and a delight to have around. No Dog Star is more open, trusting, and ready for anything. You can spring anything on an Aries dog and they'll happily jump right in, muzzle first.

IF THE ARIES DOG COULD TALK

Take me out NOW! No NOW, idiot!

I'm counting to ten and then I'm leaving without you.

I'm bored.

I want to be a macho man.

I'M right, you're wrong!

Me! Me! Me! Me!

Walk faster!

Can't touch this!

Excuuuuse me, but I was here first.

You're so slow, mo!

WHAT AN ARIES DOG WANTS IN AN OWNER

HOT DIGGETY HUMAN

Boy, I could sure dig a high-energy human to keep up with my pace. If you should have a pair of numchucks in case the neighborhood dogs get out of control, even

✳

better (devilish grin.) Will you wrestle with me often and always let me win? (Not that I wouldn't take you out on my own.) Please never, never ever make me wait for my walks or liver treats because instant gratification is my middle name. Show your love for me in obvious ways—in fact, why not have a tattoo of my name on your biceps? The more you like to shout out your love to me in public, the more I'll bark yours. Blatant displays of worship and admiration of yours truly are highly encouraged.

BARK YOUR MIND

I like an owner who says it exactly how he means it and out loud—especially if there's a chance of stirring up a little brawl. If you let me dominate the scene at the dog run without cramping my style, you're a-okay. And please buy me bright red, flashy dog collars with spikes for my birthday. Sleeping is not your thing, right? We need to share the belief that life is now or never—there's too many competitions to conquer and medals to be won. You must have enough energy to keep up with me when I dart off after my next conquest. I don't always watch where I'm going and need you to hold the leash when I forget to look both ways before rampaging across the street. I trust that you would never try to tame my fiery spirit with something as scary as obedience training—education is *so* overrated. I live by sheer instinct and raw energy, baby. Life is a battlefield and you and I are comrades in arms.

As fierce and independent as I may seem, I'm also a sucker for grand displays of affection. You'd better give me enough attention so everyone knows I'm your number-one priority, like doing everything I want when and how I want it. I'll be your hero and I expect you to be mine. You could be a firefighter or a cop, just as long as you let me break the rules and jump the fence. I thrive on danger and need constant excitement. Let's go watch the burning building or look for an accident scene just for kicks. You encourage lots of running around and barking and you'll even rage on with me—the louder you are, the better. I need a childlike owner: stuffy adults need not apply.

HOW TO EARN BROWNIE POINTS
FROM AN ARIES DOGGIE

Lots of action!	20 pts
Doggie competition	20 pts
Wrestling	20 pts
Exciting activities	20 pts
Lots of bouncy and chewy toys	20 pts
	100 pts

COMPATIBILITY GUIDE

Most Compatible with: Gemini, Leo, Sagittarius, and Aquarius

AN ARIES DOG WITH AN ARIES OWNER

Lock up the firearms and make sure you have 911 on speed-dial! This explosive combo comes complete with loud shouting and barking matches, as well as major head butting. Both human and dog think they're the bomb—and the boss. On their own, the dog and human might be a couple of pipsqueaks, but together even Godzilla is going down. When these Evil Knievels have taken out the block, they'll wrestle each other for the last beef jerky. Life is one high-speed adventure that neither will want to end. Accidents aside, this match might be hell on six legs but they're just so darn much fun to be with.

An Aries Dog with a Taurus Owner

The Taurus human may seem to have endless patience, but the Aries dog can push her to the brink. The Taurus human is solid and no-nonsense, making her the perfect owner to tame this Tasmanian devil dog. The Taurus owner needs to rest but an Aries dog's idea of rest is running around the house at a slower speed. When it comes to calming the endless zip and zap of the Aries canine's crack personality, the steady and grounded Bull has no problem enforcing discipline and consistency. Plus, the Taurus human voice is just so soothing, the Aries actually feels relaxed just being near its beloved owner.

An Aries Dog with a Gemini Owner

The Aries/Gemini pair runs on the same supersonic battery power, endlessly recharging itself when everyone else is running on empty. An Aries dog needs a smooth talker like a Gemini owner to get them both out of trouble when Animal Control shows up (again); a Gemini owner needs a whip-smart companion like an Aries dog to drag around as both accessory and bait-and-switch decoy. Together, these two are like Thelma and Louise and Starsky and Hutch wrapped into one.

AN ARIES DOG WITH A CANCER OWNER

A Cancer owner loves to dote on her little baby, if not cater to his every whim. The Aries dog is like, "Say what?! Stop cramping my style, Ma." The Cancer human may tire of an Aries dog's endless antics and household accidents, but she'll never stop babying her pride and joy. While the Aries dog hates to be cooped up, the Cancer human will gladly spend a night at home. The Cancer needs to have a big backyard to let the Aries dog tire himself out. Not one for social niceties, an Aries dog thinks he is showing his love and bravado by tearing up everything in sight. As long as he stays away from the cherished family photo album, the Cancer will continue to shower him with the baby gibberish he so adores. An Aries dog may always have the upper paw in this relationship, but no one is complaining as long as there are equal amounts of Monster Truck outings for the Aries dog and AMC movie marathons for the Cancer human.

AN ARIES DOG WITH A LEO OWNER

Look out: These two hotshots are *taking over* from LA to the Big Apple. They have a bicoastal, transcontinental following because they're born megastars who know how to get themselves on the map. Problems might arise when they have to share the spotlight; while the Leo human needs all the attention, the Aries has a bigger bark. A Leo owner may want to keep the Aries in its rightful place—the dog carrier—but in time he'll learn that there's always more room at the top. Besides, there is too much excitement to stir up with their personality-plus pooch. The Leo human quickly learns that his dynamite dog will guarantee them continued A-list status.

✳

AN ARIES DOG WITH A VIRGO OWNER

The in-your-face Aries dog is likely to give Miss Manners Virgo some serious GI trouble. The Virgo needs her pet to watch his p's and q's, while the Aries dog has manners like the Terminator. The Virgo's neat Container Store–inspired home can soon become a war zone with an Aries doggie in the house. The wildfire energy of Aries quickly topples over the neatest of piles and the sturdiest of dishes. While the Aries dog doesn't have an ounce of patience for the Virgo's fastidious ways, a "vacation" at obedience school can help.

AN ARIES DOG WITH A LIBRA OWNER

The Libra human appreciates the feisty Aries pup but also fears her attraction to all things breakable or chewable like fine pottery and furry slippers; despite his *likely* featherweight, this little dog will tip, if not flip, the Libra scales completely upside down. If the Libra human can't make up his mind, the Aries dog has no problems making it for him: he'll just (figuratively) push the wishy-washy Libra right into oncoming traffic. The Libra's sense of balance is totally destroyed by their Terminator doggie's tantrums. Libra may have to learn to bite back or at least feign growling to keep the Aries dog in check.

AN ARIES DOG WITH A SCORPIO OWNER

The calm reserve of the Scorpio human is like a good shot of Ritalin for the hyperactive Aries pooch. The Aries bites and the Scorpio stings—whereas the Scorpio human will wait for the perfect moment to fight, an Aries dog has no patience and will run headlong into battle, yapping all the way. This horrifies

✳

the Scorpio's strategic sensibilities, and the Aries dog can learn from his steady owner. In fact, the Scorpio might be the only sign of the zodiac with the power to command Aries to sit, heel, and stop barking for two seconds. But when it comes to high-energy shenanigans, this passionate pairing knows how to have a total blast.

An Aries Dog with a Sagittarius Owner

The Aries and Sagittarius share the same deep-seated fear: missing out on something. Both are the first to the party and the last to leave, and dog and owner are happy to do something (anything!) rather than stay inside. This is a cosmic pair: An Aries dog is not easily offended, so the Sag human has much leeway to insert foot in mouth; and the sports-loving Sag human will make a new religion out of watching his Aries pet chase the neighbor's dog. Between the two of them sniffing out the competition and new adventures, they'll leave no party unturned.

An Aries Dog with a Capricorn Owner

This perky pooch will either lighten up *the* serious-minded Capricorn human— or drive her batty. Most likely the latter, so be forewarned. The Capricorn owner is just the human to teach the impatient Aries pup about the hard-knock life, and the Aries dog could surely use some lessons in delayed gratification, or at least in looking before he smashes into the coffee table—again. The question is, Does the Capricorn have the time and patience to discipline this unruly Aries renegade? If the Cap human is burning the midnight oil for promotion to CEO or just too practical to shell out the money for training, there might just be a call for an emergency evacuation from the premises. But the Capricorn human is too responsible and devoted, so of course she'd actually get the best dog trainer in town to discipline her lovable but unruly Rover.

AN ARIES DOG WITH AN AQUARIUS OWNER

You can spot this eccentric dog-human couple a mile away. The Aries dog's macho groove is the perfect complement to the zany Aquarius human's mohawk and ubiquitous tattoos. The Aries dog needs constant excitement; the Aquarius human has a circuslike entourage of freaks and geeks in every city. While the Aries dog may embarrass the cool-as-a-cucumber Aquarius human with his gush attack on total strangers, the Aquarius owner doesn't really care what people think anyway. Together they're breaking the rules as they go along.

AN ARIES DOG WITH A PISCES OWNER

Pushy punk Aries will spot an instant sucker in the sacrificing Pisces human. This little ninja dog might bulldoze the Pisces owner if she's not well caffeinated. An Aries might be the only Dog Star that can get the Pisces human out of bed in the morning without hitting the snooze alarm; the Pisces human might be the only one to lure the Aries insomniac dog into counting sheep instead of chasing them. And a Pisces human could use their own little furry alarm clock anyway to get them out from under the covers. If these two can simply swap their mutually exclusive preferences for fight versus flight, the adrenaline rush is well worth the ride.

TYPICAL ARIES BREEDS

Dachshund, Chihuahua, and Jack Russell Terrier

STAR SIGHTING: FRANK—DACHSHUND

A BIG personality trapped in a little body, this bold and fiery ram can take on a dog ten or twenty times its size—at least that's what this wiener thinks. Lively and courageous, dachshunds were originally bred to dig out badgers and foxes from their dens underground. Today a popular city companion the world over, this hot dog is a fiercely passionate, affectionate, proud, independent, tenacious, boisterous, curious, and mischievous clown who knows how to keep everything under his control. Don't let his size fool you: He may easily become your master before you know it. Of course you won't really be aware of the power struggle until he's already in charge because the dachshund is clever and cute enough to mystify the smartest human. Who cares, anyway? The important thing is that everyone is happy.

Dachshunds are best with older and considerate children, and can be protective of their family. Slightly jealous and easily irritated, they're picky about other pets they hang out with. Dachshunds that are raised with siblings or other pets will have more tolerance for other animals, but like the typical Aries, this Alpha is going to be the lead singer of the band or there won't be any band at all. For the most part, the dachshund brings a bundle of joy and laughter everywhere, and you can't help but love the little wiener.

✳

REAL LIFE EXAMPLES OF DACHSHUND/ ARIES TRAITS

- Frank is a darling when no other four-legged animal is around.
- Frank's archenemies around his block include a rottweiler, bernese mountain dog, Weimaraner and any newcomers over eighty pounds. He's just waiting for the day when his mom and dad stop getting in the way; he's seriously ready to pounce on all of them.
- Watching Frank try to take on the block is enough to make everyone burst into laughter.

DOG STAR

Taurus

(A p r i l   2 0 – M a y   2 0)

THE TAURUS DOG

ELEMENT: Earth

MODALITY: Fixed

RULERSHIP: Venus

SYMBOL: Bull

MOST COMPATIBLE WITH: Virgo, Capricorn, Cancer, Pisces

WHAT A TAURUS DOG DAYDREAMS ABOUT: snuggling up with you on the couch, under a tree and snacking; chewing on a bone that never seems to end

KEYWORDS: loyal, stubborn, protective, devoted, tenacious, lazy, steady, indulgent, a foodie, simple, strong, predictable, habitual

THE TAURUS DOG STAR'S PERSONALITY

- ♉ The Taurus dog lives for the good life.
- ♉ The Taurus dog is the supreme listener and will never get tired of listening to the same stories over and over again.
- ♉ The Taurus dog is the guru of patience.
- ♉ The Taurus dog knows that good food comes to those who wait.
- ♉ The Taurus dog will never let you down.
- ♉ The Taurus dog is the consummate couch potato.
- ♉ The Taurus dog cannot be bullied into changing his position on things.
- ♉ The Taurus dog loves steady routine.
- ♉ The Taurus dog knows there is nothing worth rushing for.
- ♉ The Taurus dog needs a slow tempo and a large dog bowl.

STAR SIGN CHARACTERISTICS

THE HUNGRY AND LOYAL POOCH

The perpetually famished Taurus dog may rob you of your stash of Frito-Lay's but his undying devotion to you will also steal your heart away. His loyalty is unmatched: He'll see every obstacle through until the end, no matter how arduous the journey. You would never have to be concerned about the Taurus dog "cheating" on you—it's rare that a Taurus doggie would even take a second look at another potential owner unless, of course, that person happens to own a restaurant.

SUPERSIZE ME

The Taurus dog lives for large portions of food—both of the dog and people food varieties. Okay, so he's a little greedy and doesn't take kindly to sharing his food, but you'd better be prepared to share yours. (Cut him some slack, a Taurus dog has the biggest appetite of the zodiac!) He'll expect to eat whenever you do, so try to plan your meals accordingly to avoid the big bark of this eternally hungry little badger dog. Regularity in both feeding and walking schedules is key in keeping the Taurus pooch a happy camper. It might be wise to trick your pup into thinking that he is eating more by cutting down portion size and feeding him little healthy treats throughout the day. The good news is that this Dog Star possesses plenty of patience and accepts delayed gratification—he can be trained to wait patiently for his regular mealtimes. The downside is, should you fall off schedule by even a few minutes the Taurus dog will let you know it in no uncertain terms. The Taurus pooch has no shame when it comes to barking loudly for on-demand feeding.

COUCH POTATO

After a good hearty meal, it's siesta time for the Taurus doggie. This Dog Star knows how to max and relax, and was sent to you by the stars to teach you the fine art of doing nothing. The Taurus dog hates to be rushed and even worse to be called the L-word, as in *lazy*. Lounging *is* an art form perfected by this Venus-ruled pup. He cannot be pushed into doing anything against his strong will, and should you decide to get all bossy on your little Taurus friend, watch him dig in his heels. He needs gentle coaxing to get from dog bed to food bowl to sidewalk, and gets very attached to routine. He prefers a steady, predictable day of indulgent rituals like mealtime, treat time, nap time, and massage time. You can bet your bottom dollar, this dog will teach you some serious lessons in punctuality.

TAKE THIS WALK AND SHOVE IT

While most dogs jump for joy when they hear the word *walk,* don't expect your Taurus doggie to have any natural inclination to move from the comfy confines of his dog bed. The Taurus doggie is more likely to feign sleep or pretend he doesn't feel well to avoid changing positions from lying down to standing on all fours. Walking is just another annoying chore to this leisurely pup: Exerting himself is not his idea of a good time. The Taurus dog prefers chewing on his favorite bone or snuggling with you. Exercise schmexercise, what are a few extra pounds?

STUBBORN BULL

Watch his happy-dappy doggie spirit dwindle in seconds when you take away the Taurus dog's favorite toy. He won't surrender his prized possessions or treats without putting up a major tug-of-war with you either. The Taurus is perhaps the most fiercely stubborn and determined canine Dog Star of the zodiac. No matter how many hours and dollars you pour into obedience training, this cutie may refuse to learn to respond to "let go." He gets very attached to things, and will hold on for dear life. The good news is that he'll never tire of snuggling with you, even if he insists on hogging all the blankets.

IF THE TAURUS DOG COULD TALK

Life is meant for relaxation.

What's the big rush?

Can't make me do it.

Can you please walk a little slower? I'm winded already.

Take time to smell the flowers. Jeeez.

Lean on me: I'm solid as a rock!

All I want is food and love and more food.

Can't you hear my stomach growling?

Supersize fries only come in one size?

Don't forget about my daily full-body massage before you fall asleep!

WHAT A TAURUS DOG WANTS IN AN OWNER

FOODIE AND LAZY BOY

Do you appreciate good food and just kicking back in your easy chair? If so, you're my kind of mommy or daddy! I can't deal with huffy, pushy humans who

✳

lack gentleness and patience. I also don't dig fakes or showoffs, so spare me if you're one of those wannabe poser types. I don't like fluff. I am the real McCoy and I want an owner who is as genuine and down to earth as I am. Y'know, a real meat and potatoes kind of man or woman to call my very own. Okay, so I'm a little possessive over my mommy or daddy. In my heart of hearts, I yearn for that special someone who will spoil me rotten. Oh, and of course it's important that you're the kind of someone who understands the importance of fluffy pillows, a big bone, lots of snacks, and endless affection.

MARRIAGE

Furthermore, I, Taurus doggie, expect loyalty because Lord knows I'm going to put every fiber of my canine being into our relationship "'til death do us part." Please give me an owner who isn't fickle. I need someone who sees every obstacle through with patience and perseverance, who understands my distaste for change: and that includes changing my dog food, my bed, or my short (keyword: short) little walks around the block. Sudden shifts in plans make me insecure and grouchy: I need stability, reliability, and an owner who's solid as a rock. Throwing off my rhythm is the worst thing you can do, so if you're one of those flaky, changeable types, please sign up for a time management course. Otherwise you'll make me so nervous I'll resort to oversleeping or binge eating just to deal with the lack of routine and the chaos. Maybe you should know that I simply do not thrive in mutable environments. Consistency is key. I need the kind of owner I can set my watch by. I need to know that you'll always come through, right on time like you said you would: a true-blue best friend, loyal and devoted to the core.

FRIEND OF NATURE

If you live near the woods, or live in a log cabin, even better. I love trees and nature. At least take me to the park or let me sniff around the flowers at a nearby garden if you don't have one of your own. Flowers make me almost as happy as food. I need fresh air and life at a slower pace than the average dog. I'm not really a city dog because I don't adapt well to all of the hustle and bustle and the lack of greenery. Movers and shakers, and surprises are so not my thing—save them for my Aquarian Dog Star cousins. I prefer a rural setting, but if that's not possible, surround me with a tranquil environment and frequent trips to the country. It's important for me to stay grounded. I also prefer if you have a fat bank account because lack of funds does not bode well for my sense of security. If the stash of dog food starts to run low I may panic, so it's advisable to always have an extra supply on hand—it gives me a wonderful sense of that safety blanket I so crave.

HOW TO EARN BROWNIE POINTS
FROM A TAURUS DOGGIE

Lots and lots of food	20 pts
Lots and lots of treats	20 pts
Daily full body massages	20 pts
Slow and short walks	20 pts
Cushy and comfy dog bed	20 pts
	100 pts

COMPATIBILITY GUIDE

Most Compatible with: Virgo, Capricorn, Cancer, Pisces

A TAURUS DOG WITH AN ARIES OWNER

A hothead and a stubborn mule make for a cantankerous pairing, but the truth is you have so much to learn from one another. The go-go Aries human loses patience with the Taurus dog's leisurely ways. The Taurus doggie feels stressed out by the type A tendencies of the Aries human. These two are seriously out of sync but the point is to learn from each other. A Taurus dog could use a little Arian pep, and the Aries human could learn the fine art of delayed gratification and patience. Taurus doggies are like a nice shot of Valium for the Aries humans.

A TAURUS DOG WITH A TAURUS OWNER

A veritable meeting of the clean-plate club! Who better to indulge in the comforts of life than your very own Taurus dream dog? Finally, a being as loyal, patient and tranquil as you are. Yes, this pair might mirror their own stubborn, habit-forming ways. Yes, they both love to indulge beyond reasonable limits. Yes, they both have their comfy little ruts that they know they'd be better off without. And yes, they're both great at the art of relaxation. Taurus and Taurus together guarantees that life is rich, relaxing, and savory! Bon appétit!

A TAURUS DOG WITH A GEMINI OWNER

The whimsical Gemini might find the predictable Taurus poochie a stick in the mud. Likewise, a steadfast Taurus might find an ADD Gemini a scary prospect as a dependable caretaker. The Gemini humans are usually too busy multitasking to remember they even have a dog, let alone a dog that needs to be walked, and especially fed. The Gemini human might get sick of fighting with her stubborn little bull who refuses to run around town at a moment's notice. But this dependable little anchor is exactly what a mercurial Gemini needs. It's the solid grounding that will do wonders for helping a Gemini human follow through and stick to the plan. The Gemini might even slow down and smell the roses.

A TAURUS DOG WITH A CANCER OWNER

Sweet and comforting as mom's homemade apple pie, the Cancer human is the perfect candidate as the steady-freddy Taurus dog's caretaker. Both love someone they can truly count on, and both detest surprises. Both love to lounge around at home. Both love a good home-cooked meal. Both are very possessive and security-oriented. They'll feel safe and cozy together. With so much at-home hiding out, it's a good thing Taurus dogs tend to have bladders of steel.

A TAURUS DOG WITH A LEO OWNER

Rivalry and control issues breed excitement and spur both the Taurus dog and the Leo owner on to their stubborn bests. But deep down they both love the challenge and would actually do anything for each other. The Taurus dog wants his way or the highway. The Leo human believes the world must revolve around her and only her. If you can reach an agreement to play fan club for the other, there could be some good mutual ego stroking in this combo. If concessions can be made when necessary, the clash of your control-freak ways could have mucho rewards.

✳

A TAURUS DOG WITH A VIRGO OWNER

This relationship is no-nonsense, and simplicity at its best. The Virgo human will have no problem with a Taurus dog's need for routine because she is equally ritualistic and fanatical when it comes to serving her beloved pet. The hyperresponsible Virgo will never fail to miss a beat when it comes to proper feeding and grooming. The Taurus pooch feels safe as a bug in a rug with this conscientious nutritionist. The vet is sure to be impressed.

A TAURUS DOG WITH A LIBRA OWNER

The Taurus doggie just adores how the Libra human creates so much beauty in its world. Venus rules both so it's no wonder they have such similar taste. Both are gentle and peace-loving. Both understand the importance of relaxation and meditation. Both live for love, serenity, and the perfect gourmet meal—with white chocolate cheesecake drenched in raspberry sauce for dessert, of course. This little duo is pure sweetness and light—just look out for the inevitable cavities to follow. They also tend to bring out each other's lazy side.

A TAURUS DOG WITH A SCORPIO OWNER

Ain't no mountain high enough, no river wide enough to keep these two apart. Even if they stubbornly fight for the driver's seat with no intention of backing down, unless they crash into a telephone pole they'll make up in the end. They bring out the decadence and indulgence in each other so it won't be a surprise if they both gain a little poundage. They're both die-hard-loyal to the core and will stand by each other against the rest of the flimsy world.

A Taurus Dog with a Sagittarius Owner

The fun potential outweighs the odd couple aspects between the Taurus dog and Sag human. The Sag can't possibly expect the Taurus dog to suddenly break out of his slowpoke pace, but he can help the Taurus doggie break out of his ruts and comfort zones by luring him into wild adventures and crazy convertible rides at high speeds. The Taurus dog feels eternally youthful, like a gypsy spirit on the road, with his sagelike Sag counterpart. And the Sag feels wonderfully safe and secure knowing he has his little Rock of Gibraltar best friend always by his side.

A Taurus Dog with a Capricorn Owner

When it comes to the nitty-gritty, nuts and bolts of life, the Taurus dog and the Capricorn human set the bar high for others to follow. They have a fat bank account because they know how to save by buying dog food in bulk. A Taurus loves anything in bulk. He can also set his doggie watch by the Capricorn's strict adherence to regular walks and mealtimes. Together they get the job done, the bills paid, and the dog bowl clean.

A Taurus Dog with an Aquarian Owner

While the Aquarius human is off in some genius future, the Taurus dog is dying to be fed in the here and now. The Taurus doggie wants the Aquarian human to come down from the astral plane and share some spuds. However, the Aquarius cannot always be reached on the astral plane. She doesn't do anything in a predictable fashion and a Taurus doggie thrives on knowing what comes next. The Aquarius human's eccentric nature makes the Taurus overeat. This is one creature

✳

the Aquarius can't figure out. Why doesn't the Taurus dog have loftier ambitions like saving the world? But in the end, they can become an inseparable duo because they share the most important thing in common: They make the best friends.

A TAURUS DOG WITH A PISCES OWNER

Both spend most of their time fast asleep. That's the good news. The bad news is that the Pisces has the terrible habit of hitting the snooze button way beyond the Taurus dog's feeding time. The Taurus dog will feel like he's drowning in deep, murky waters in this messy Piscean household where the dog food dries up and the leash is in the water bowl. But the Taurus can help the Pisces get some much-needed structure and discipline, and since the Pisces would sacrifice anything for those she loves, she'll happily change her ways for the beloved little Taurus poochie.

TYPICAL TAURUS BREEDS

Bulldog, Bassett Hound, French Bulldog, and Saint Bernard

STAR SIGHTING: MO—BULLDOG

One does not have to be an astrologer to figure this one out. Duh . . . Taurus, the Bull? Originally bred for bull and bear baiting, the stocky bulldog is bold, aware, and courageous despite his lethargic nature. If you don't mind the bullheaded stubbornness of this slow-moving companion, a bulldog, like a typical Taurus,

will be devoted, loyal, kind, loving, and affectionate. The bulldog has a very soothing quality that can put his owners at ease. Comfort and relaxation—that's the bulldog's motto. If you're looking for a friend to calm you down or lower your blood pressure, the bulldog is for you! Or if you're a couch potato and want a warm footrest, the bulldog will happily accommodate.

Like all other canine companions, this lazy pup does have some problems. It may not be wise for a light sleeper to pick this big snorer unless you keep him outside of your bedroom. And if you're not a fan of sloppy, wet kisses, be forewarned: Bulldogs have a problem with saliva control.

REAL-LIFE EXAMPLES OF BULLDOG/ TAURUS TRAITS

- One of Mo's favorite hangouts is the local firehouse, where he gets plenty of love and affection from the superheroes. During our location scout for Mo, he went straight into the firehouse and refused to leave like a stubborn bull. (See photo)
- Mo missed his appointment to look at his own beauty shots because he was too comfortable on the couch; his mommy could not drag him out.
- See for yourself at a local dog run: Chances are, the bulldogs won't be going anywhere. They will most likely be lying in a shady spot.

DOG STAR

Gemini

(M a y   2 1 – J u n e   2 0)

THE GEMINI DOG

ELEMENT: Air

MODALITY: Mutable

RULERSHIP: Mercury

SYMBOL: The Twins

MOST COMPATIBLE WITH: Libra, Aquarius, Aries, Leo

WHAT A GEMINI DOG DAYDREAMS ABOUT: Running all over town with you from bookstore to café; a weekend getaway

KEYWORDS: unpredictable, versatile, smart, sociable, high-energy, curious, easily distracted, restless, dual

> ## THE GEMINI DOG STAR'S PERSONALITY
>
> ♊ The Gemini dog wants to run around town with you.
>
> ♊ The Gemini dog needs to be in the know.
>
> ♊ The Gemini dog wants you to be their twin.
>
> ♊ The Gemini dog loves newspapers, magazines, and TV.
>
> ♊ The Gemini dog is eternally youthful.
>
> ♊ The Gemini dog likes to play games with you and trick you.
>
> ♊ The Gemini dog is the ultimate trendsetter of the zodiac.

STAR SIGN CHARACTERISTICS

TRAINS, PLANES, AND DOGGIE CARRIERS

See that charming and youthful-looking Dog Star running around like a planet on speed? Yep, must be a Gemini pup. This magpie of a dog loves to chat it up and gives the phrase *on the go* new meaning. So much to see and do, so little time! So much to say and so few ways to bark it! This is one of the brightest and most adaptable doggies of the zodiac. More than any other sign, they can easily adjust to almost any situation. If you're a jetsetter yourself—jackpot!—because these doggie dilettantes love, love, *love* to travel. They are happiest when in transit with their beloved twin star (that's you, of course). Whether in a train, car, or airplane, Gemini dogs find travel sheer bliss. This is one dog sign that shouldn't need any doggie tranquilizers—unless, of course, there is some kind of odd affliction to their stars. Typical Gem Dog Stars adore nothing more than being in perpetual motion and seeing the world. In case you haven't noticed, they're also multilingual so don't try to sneak anything past them in another language because you simply won't get away with it.

I Think, Therefore I Am Dog

The Gemini Dog Star loves people and, quite honestly, wishes it could chat it up with everyone over a gin and tonic. Watch the wheels turning in the little Gemini dog's head: They're busy dreaming up a million brilliant schemes and tricks to be played on unsuspecting humans. This dog lives for fun and games—especially games. Gemini dogs bore easily because their minds are always on to the next thing; they lose their focus very easily. You'll have to give them plenty of variety to keep their little noggins stimulated—the more things happening simultaneously the better. They're even into playing catch and reading a book at the same time. Oh, don't think that they haven't learned to read just because they're of the canine species. If Gemini pups could hold a pen they'd probably write an entire novel. They love to have stories read to them at bedtime, too. If you're not an avid reader, they also enjoy watching television or listening to the radio with you—or both at the same time. The Gemini loves music: as long as it's not Muzak or anything outdated, they'll pretty much dig it and probably dance around the house with you. They're great mimics. They'll even take on some of your mannerisms. They live to entertain and make people laugh. They'll gladly perform tricks, stand on two legs, catch, shake—you name it. And they are perhaps the fastest learners in the doggie zodiac.

DR. JEKYLL AND MR. RAWHIDE

Soon you might begin to notice that this smarty-pants pooch seems to have not one but at least two rather distinct personalities. Your Gemini pup might even appear to walk in two directions at once—or first to the right and then to left—when they're rambling down the sidewalk sniffing everything and everyone in sight. Why walk in a straight line when zigzag fashion is so much fun? The Gemini doesn't want to miss out on anything. You'll soon ask yourself: Is this little Gemini child of mine an angel or a devil? One day your little dog star is perfectly innocent, cute, cuddly, full of zing; and the next he or she is a holy terror leaving one disaster after another in their wake. This little trickster doggie can't resist a little mischief now and then. They get a thrill out of stealing little objects from other dogs or even you, so if something comes up missing be sure to find out where your pooch keeps his loot.

NAUGHTY BY NATURE

How boring to have only one persona: it's all about double trouble, double the pleasure with their twin self. Try your best to understand and love both sides equally to prevent the Gemini doggie from going loco on you with a split personality. If you can't play the role of soul mate and twin for your Gemini pup, you might want to consider getting them a little sibling. They feel better with a counterpart, a partner in fun and in crime. If you can't be that for them, they may sneak out of the house to find someone who will. Be sure to always have an ID tag on your wandering pooch because they thrive on getting lost—and they're sneaky enough to escape. Keep them endlessly supplied with toys or their

*

restless minds could easily tempt them into stirring up some trouble, like messing up your house or hiding your favorite pair of slippers. Born tricksters, these clever little canines can't resist pulling a few over on their beloved owners now and then.

WHICH WAY DID I GO—WHICH WAY DID I GO?

The doggie multitaskers, the Gemini pups confuse easily because they are constantly taking in the multifarious stimuli bombarding them from every direction. They don't want to miss a beat. They just have a hard time making up their mind about what they want to sniff, or when they want to eat, or which way they want to walk. They will probably defer to you for the answers because all the back and forth, Ping-Pong volleying in their little doggie brains is too much sometimes. Even if they seem to contradict your wishes, rest assured that you are helping to ease their fear of decision making. It's easier for them to contradict you than to make up their own minds. So just pull in the reins a little tighter and watch how you instantly seem to quell their anxiety. All of their running around (even while sleeping they are dreaming of running around!) very often keeps these dogs slim no matter how much food they eat. They burn off a lot of calories with their constant hyperactivity. These trendy dogs are style savvy, too. They're born hipsters, setting the trends for the other dogs in the 'hood to follow. Your Gemini pup could easily end up on the front page of the next chic dog magazine. They were born for the media, darling, and know how to work the camera and an interview like no other Dog Star, except maybe Leo.

✳

IF THE GEMINI DOG COULD TALK

Here I am now—entertain me!

Let's play hide and seek.

What? Huh?

Wait, where did I hide my bone?

Wanna hear some gossip?

What's that? I want to see! Let me see!

Why? But why? But why? Why?

Tell me a good story or a good joke.

I don't wanna grow up!

More toys, new toys, this is so lame!

WHAT A GEMINI DOG WANTS IN AN OWNER

SIR MIX-A-LOT

I prefer an owner who likes to mix it up in life: you know, someone who keeps things interesting. I need constant stimulation and gads of fascinating people coming in and out of the house! The more buzz, the better. My owner has to be a lively character who loves to travel and will take me with him (or at least let me sleep in my pet carrier and pretend I am traveling even if it's just in my dreams). I love you if you're cute as a button and smart as a whip: 'cos I am. If you like to go to parties and hang out in cool local spots in our neighborhood—and of course take me with you every time—then you rock.

ME AND MR. A.D.D.

Do you like to play music and watch television at the same time? Or read magazines and watch television at the same time? Do crossword puzzles or read out loud? All these things I find immensely comforting. Will you let me multitask? Can we go roller skating with our headphones on? Will you take me to see the world? Will you teach me lots of new tricks? You'd better be funny and sly or you'll bore me to tears. I need someone who can love both of my twins. I need someone who doesn't care that I don't walk a straight line in life. You understand the value of going in circles to chase your own tail: just because, just because you can. I admire an owner with a great sense of humor and the charm of eternal youth. If you share my curiosity about life and even like to read the tabloids, I think we'll get on famously.

HOW TO EARN BROWNIE POINTS
FROM A GEMINI DOGGIE

New toys	20 pts
Frequent outings	20 pts

Fun activities	20 pts
Road trips	20 pts
Parties	20 pts
	100 pts

COMPATIBILITY GUIDE

Most Compatible with: Libra, Aquarius, Aries, Leo

A GEMINI DOG WITH AN ARIES OWNER

This dog-human combo rocks the party. Both of you are wild and crazy and will love spending time chasing rainbows and cuties down the block; a Gemini dog's insatiable curiosity goes well with an Aries's love of adventure. You both have more energy than a nuclear generator and will forever keep each other on your toes—or paws. You share the philosophy "the early bird catches the worm." Hence, lack of sleep might be the only issue because neither of you is willing to settle down first. You both share the big fear of "missing out" on something, so rest is not usually an option.

A GEMINI DOG WITH A TAURUS OWNER

A Taurus human will be tempted to send the Gemini back to the animal shelter after a mere two hours with this yahoo of a doggie; but their loyal nature will make it hard for the Taurus to throw in the towel. A Gemini doggie gets bored so easily with the steadfast Taurus, they will have no choice but to stir things up by stealing the Taurus human's shoes, socks, and other prized possessions. Such antics leave the Bull seeing nothing but red. But the bottom line is you need each other to keep life both grounded and interesting. But we pity the fool who tries to steal the Taurus human's prized possessions or food. That doggie may very well be exported back to their country of origin.

A Gemini Dog with a Gemini Owner

Twins, together at last! What a crazy duo you make; you'll just have to ignore the people who say "There goes the neighborhood," when they see the two of you scheming your latest prank. Life is a nonstop cabaret with all of the mercurial energy between you. Only which one of you will play good twin and which will play the evil one? And how will you ever figure out which way to go on walks? You're bound to get confused: both of you are such tricksters, so who gets punked? Actually, who cares?! You'll have such a hoot together that it won't even matter who gets the last laugh or howl.

A Gemini Dog with a Cancer Owner

The Cancer will get aggravated with Gemini's constant need to be out on the town. What could be better than staying at home? The Cancer human gets grumpy with the Gemini dog's tricks and pranks and endless charades. A Cancer doesn't understand why a Gemini has to run around in strange patterns but finds it pretty darn cute and amusing. Plus, a Cancer human needs someone to get them to leave the lure of their nest once in awhile. A Gemini dog just wants to help the Cancer human break out of their shell and even meet new and bizarre friends—this however, is not the Cancer's idea of a good time.

A GEMINI DOG WITH A LEO OWNER

The most dynamite trendsetters of the zodiac, you both know how to work the limelight. You two press darlings have a revolving fan club of adolescent admirers. You're both born red-carpet divas who look like you have your own personal stylist—and chances are, you actually do. Life is all about showing off and collecting the accolades. The Leo human will take pride in his pup's precocious brain. You're so fabulous together; you might even score your own reality TV show.

A GEMINI DOG WITH A VIRGO OWNER

Both dog and human are worrywarts and make each other jumpy, but it'll save you both money on the daily venti lattes. You'll keep each other naturally revved up. You'll find you love running errands together because you get so much done so quickly. A Gemini dog enjoys running around town while an industrious, efficient Virgo completes the little tasks. The Virgo human makes sure the Gemini dog always has the latest and best outfits and carriers to tool around in. Plus, the Virgo human likes to take the Gemini pooch to work and Gemini loves being around all the action and the opportunity for great people-watching. And the to-do lists always get done!

A GEMINI DOG WITH A LIBRA OWNER

Bona fide social butterflies, you'll enjoy flitting around together. A Gemini dog loves to flirt as much as a Libra human and you'll both love being used as a decoy to snag their latest crush. Both love variety and travel; the only issue is, both of you are so indecisive you'll have trouble figuring out where to go and what to do. Perhaps the best plan is to always have at least two options available: like going to the pet store and the ice-cream shop, to avoid any potential regrets. Together you find ways to have your cake and eat it, too!

A Gemini Dog with a Scorpio Owner

Try as they might, A Gemini dog will have a hard time getting anything past a Scorpio's X-ray vision. The Gemini doggie will soon get bored and start looking for other outlets for their restless energy. The Scorpio human wishes chatty Gemini would simmer down on the barking. The Gemini doggie wants to go out for marathon walks during reasonable hours when the other dogs go out but the Scorpio human will only go on midnight walks. The Scorpio human wants Gemini all to himself or herself. But there is some serious healing potential in this combo, because the curious Gemini pooch is never bored with an eccentric Scorpio human, and vice versa. Your best compatibility can be found in your love for extremes.

A Gemini Dog with a Sagittarius Owner

For Sag and Gemini, life is a bowl of Neapolitan ice cream, an endless block party, and a nonstop flight to Barbados. You'll never know if you're coming or going and you'll probably forget to eat. But that's just the way you like it. Everyone will be attracted to this bon vivant pairing because clearly you know where the fun is to be found. Plus, both of you have boundless energy and instantly lift the spirits of anyone that comes within a two-foot radius of you two. The Sag human loves to play teacher and the Gemini dog adores being the teacher's pet. With all of their adventures and waxing philosophical, they're bound to discover the meaning of life.

A GEMINI DOG WITH A CAPRICORN OWNER

This misfit combo doesn't make any sense to the practical Capricorn. Capricorns are good with patience and delayed gratification but they can't understand why the Gemini doggie seems so clueless in these departments. The Capricorn human will have a hard time disciplining this rambunctious pooch—and this makes for one disgruntled Goat. To a Capricorn, things don't work without discipline and structure—and a Gemini doggie doesn't care about being practical. If only this dog would learn to walk a straight line instead of zigzaggy all over the place. If obedience school doesn't work, Cap will have no choice but to fire this pup.

A GEMINI DOG WITH AN AQUARIUS OWNER

This will be a mutual instant addiction when you both realize that you've found your cosmic partner in crime. You're both into jokes, television, people-watching, and rebelling against the status quo. Neither of you can resist playing practical jokes on the unsuspecting. You'll find enough entertainment between the two of you to never suffer from the boredom of monotony. If that doesn't work, you can always rely on each other for game show marathons. You might attract all the freaks and geeks in the neighborhood but that's just par for the course. You both celebrate the "live and let live" philosophy.

A GEMINI DOG WITH A PISCES OWNER

A Gemini doggie can't stand the typical late sleeping and avoidance tactics of the Pisces human. Why, oh, why, must we stay in and miss out on everything just because the Pisces is too drained to deal with reality? This leaves the Gemini dog with no choice but to bark Pisces out of his netherworld to go for a walk. The Pisces wishes the Gemini dog would sleep more or at least become a figment of their imagination once in awhile, for goodness' sake! Both have great imaginations and a soft spot for poetry. If the Gemini can compromise with some extra snooze time in exchange for a bedtime story, these two might find they're fairy tale material after all—or at least an interesting horror show.

TYPICAL GEMINI BREEDS

Mutt

STAR SIGHTING: DORIS
(BEAGLE—BASSETT HOUND/BEAGLE MIX)

Like a typical Gemini, this dog will keep your relationship fresh and exciting. You'll never know which twin you're getting at any given time. You might even get triplets or quadruplets. How could one little dog have so many different personalities? There's never a boring moment with this pup. If you're a free spirit who appreciates spontaneity and surprises, a mutt is your perfect match.

A Gemini often appears to be a little scattered; but that's just because it's trying to ride a bicycle while listening to hip-hop in one ear and talking on the phone on the other. If you think it can't be done, just watch a Gemini dog in action. The Twins can manage all that *and* stop for an ice-cream cone. That's the beauty of having two or more brains in one body—like a mutt—it's pure brilliance! If your mutt exhibits ADD tendencies, it's just part of the Gemini package. Mutts usually have fewer health problems than pure breeds. They are exceptional because no two mutts look or act the same—a truly irreplaceable friend!

Be sure to socialize the Gemini mutt early on with all kinds of people and dogs; that's what they live for! Flitting about, sniffing every flower and dog and person, they need constant stimulation. They'll even like dog school because they get to make new friends; plus, it's good training for these little socialites.

REAL-LIFE EXAMPLES OF MUTT/GEMINI TRAITS

- Doris manages to divide her week up between three states. During the weekdays she spends time between her home in New Jersey and her workplace, where she assists her mommy as a doggie day-care assistant in New York. On the weekends she relaxes in her country home in Pennsylvania.
- Doris's mommy received a phone call from a neighbor one day who had found Doris waiting to be served at their dining table.

DOG STAR

Cancer

(J u n e   2 1 – J u l y   2 2)

THE CANCER DOG

ELEMENT: Water

MODALITY: Cardinal

RULERSHIP: Moon

SYMBOL: Crab

MOST COMPATIBLE WITH: Scorpio. Pisces, Taurus, Virgo

WHAT A CANCER DOG DAYDREAMS ABOUT: Rainy days and snowstorms, so you'll have no interest in going outside; AMC movie marathons; listening to the radio; watching you smoke your pipe or bake apple pie

KEYWORDS: sensitive, moody, emotional, intuitive, domestic, shy, touchy, nurturing, protective, needy

THE CANCER DOG STAR'S PERSONALITY

- The Cancer dog needs to be cuddled.
- The Cancer dog needs to be mommied and says, "Home is where the heart is."
- The Cancer dog needs home-cooked food.
- The Cancer dog needs you to remember his birthday and your anniversary.
- The Cancer dog has a memory like an elephant—he never forgets.
- The Cancer dog is extremely sensitive to harsh words, so speak sweetly and softly.
- The Cancer dog likes other dogs that are as sensitive as he is.

STAR SIGN CHARACTERISTICS

YOU DON'T BRING ME FLOWERS ANYMORE

The Cancer pooch is the most sensitive and nurturing of all Dog Stars. He has a tough exterior shell but that's simply to protect his vulnerable little heart. He wants to take care of you and be babied in return. Like his symbol, the Crab, the Cancer doggie will never approach matters directly but will sidle up to you with subtle hints that he needs something. He's a home-loving pup and soooo keenly sensitive to his environment that if you live in a dumpy or an austere apartment, you should start redecorating or he'll be forced to run away from home. This domestic doggie needs to be treated like a true and cherished member of the family—not just some pet relegated to a doghouse or crate. This dog is not only sensitive—he borders on psychic. He feels it when you're going to leave him for your vacation even if you leave no clues. He'll even run and hide when he feels a vet trip in the near future—even though you've given no indication that you've booked an appointment.

C.D. (CANCER DOG) PHONE HOME

This doggie is more than just a lover of all things domestic—he is fervently attached to his home. It takes a lot to convince him that there is anything worth leaving his little sanctuary for. If he could live under a blanket away from all loud noises, people, and other doggies he probably would. He'd hope you would share this home-loving sensibility and feel it utterly unnecessary to go out. He can't stand to see you leave the home, and will wait anxiously for your return. His favorite times are cozy nights spent at home with you. He loves affection from you but can't stand strangers touching him let alone grooming him—especially if he or she is rough or aggressive. The Cancer Dog Star is so shy and sensitive on first meetings that it may surprise you how antisocial he can be. Other than his immediate family, the Cancer pup really doesn't care for strangers all that much. He'll be utterly traumatized if you throw him into a dog run with a bunch of brutish types. He needs to be around other sensitive and caring souls who approach him gently and with caution. Overzealousness makes his fur crawl.

MEMORIES, LIKE THE CORNERS OF MY MIND

This dog has a memory like an elephant and expects you to have the same, especially when it comes to remembering his birthday or the anniversary of the day you brought him home. Be sensitive to shower him with plenty of reassurance and make him feel safe and secure knowing that you'll never leave his side for long. He has an abandonment complex, after all. He'll be unduly traumatized for life if you raise your voice or even yank his leash too hard out of impatience. Things that might just roll off another Dog Star's back will leave deep lifelong scars on your thin-skinned Cancer doggie. And he may forgive, but he never, ever forgets.

LOONEY TUNES

The Cancer Dog Star is ruled by the moon, which might explain his frequent lunaticlike outbursts. Your friends and neighbors will undoubtedly marvel at the oddball behavior of your Cancer pooch—wondering where on earth you ever got such a loose-cannon creature. Just make sure they don't insult your hypersensitive pooch because the Cancer Dog Star's feelings are so easily hurt. You'll have to get used to the way your moon-ruled pup exhibits even stranger behaviors during a full moon. He may even start howling for no reason or suddenly start wolfing down his dog food on those nights. Or he may simply run around the house like a possessed little freak for no apparent reason. Blame it on *la luna*.

IF THE CANCER DOG COULD TALK

That hurt my feelings.

I want to be your baby.

I want to go home!

You forgot our anniversary!

So I get a little nutso—sue me!

I want my mommy!

Where're my homemade dog treats?

I'm feeling a little melancholy today.

I'm only happy when it rains.

I'm cranky, don't bug me.

WHAT A CANCER DOG WANTS IN AN OWNER

THERE'S NO PLACE LIKE HOME

I want someone to treat me like her little baby and make me feel I am really the most cherished member of the entire family. If you have a baby already, I will be so

✳

jealous because I want to be the child of the family. I need nurturing! I want someone who hates to leave home for any extended period of time. And don't try to fool me by packing at the last minute, because days before, I'll sense if you're leaving. Puleeez, don't abandon me or I could easily develop digestive issues. The more domestic and home loving you are, the more my little Cancerian soul will feel assured. It's all about security, lest my fur start falling out. I really need a sensitive owner who gives the kind of loving care a doting grandparent showers on their favorite grandchild. I'd prefer if you wouldn't bring strangers around the house and expect me to interact with them in some extroverted way. Ain't happening, friend—I don't like sharing my house or my owner with new people—my place, my space! I want us to hide out together in our quiet little sanctuary, safely away from the battering of the cruel outside world. And why do you have to bring any outsiders in? It makes me way uncomfortable, I'll have you know that I don't warm up to others that easily. It takes time and I have to trust someone before I'll be willing to come out of my furry shell.

HEALTHY PLEASURES
Oh, and I'd like an owner who uses all-natural cleaning and grooming products because I have a very delicate system. Chemicals make me ill. I prefer natural doggie food, too, since artificial ingredients could easily lead to major health issues, because I just mentioned, I've got a sensitive constitution. I'm also a very finicky eater—so if I don't like my dog food, I won't eat it.

BARKING AT THE MOON
I want someone who likes to go for long walks during a full moon and won't mind if I display my wacky lunar tendencies at this time. If you're into moon wor-

ship or Wicca, you'll totally rock my world. When the moon is new, I'm usually at my lowest energy. When it's waxing, I may actually agree to leave the house once in a while. When it is full, look out! I may need to do laps around the house and then bark like a psycho for the fun of it. When the moon is waning, I need my space and extra sleep time. Keeping in tune with the moon phases is key if you want to understand my wacky, lunar nature. My little doggie moods ebb and flow in accordance with the big silver ball in the sky.

HOW TO EARN BROWNIE POINTS
FROM A CANCER DOGGIE

Lots of motherly love	20 pts
Cozy home	20 pts
Homemade meals	20 pts
Homemade treats	20 pts
Romantic walks	20 pts
	100 pts

COMPATIBILITY GUIDE

Most Compatible with: Scorpio, Pisces, Taurus, Virgo

A CANCER DOG WITH AN ARIES OWNER
The Aries human's feisty spirit is the perfect pick-me-up for the introverted Cancer dog. The Aries human is a wee bit loud and proud for the needy and vulnerable

Cancer Dog Star. But the nurturing Cancer doggie helps to smooth out the Aries human's harder edges. They both love family, picnics, and carnivals. The Aries human learns the invaluable lesson of patience and emotional intelligence from the precocious Cancer pup.

A Cancer Dog with a Taurus Owner

Optimal security is the name of the game for both of you. You love staying home and watching old black-and-white movies while eating warm blueberry pie. The Taurus human is as soothing as a summer afternoon in the garden for the Cancer doggie. The Taurus is never fazed by the Cancer doggie's inexplicable mood swings; the Cancer dog revels in knowing that the Taurus human will stick to him like glue. Life is one big cozyfest when you're together.

A Cancer Dog with a Gemini Owner

The whimsical nature of the Gemini human will make the Cancer doggie nervous. A Cancer doggie doesn't have to be psychic to know that the Gemini human is about to uproot him at any second by running off to join a circus or a dance troupe and drag the Cancer doggie around from city to city. The domestic scene is just a pit stop for the Gemini human and this would be tragic for the home-obsessed Cancer doggie. The Gemini human may have no choice but to drag her Cancer pooch, kicking and barking, in a low-profile dog carrier to avoid a big scene in public.

A Cancer Dog with a Cancer Owner

A must-do pairing! Nothing could be better than two little Cancers—one human, one canine—that shack up and play house together. You'll smother each other with comfort and care and no one is going anywhere without the other one attached at the hip. This symbiotic, mushball pairing would need an eviction notice just to get them out of the house once in awhile. Sure you might grumble at each other now and then, but you both know intuitively that it's just a passing mood.

A CANCER DOG WITH A LEO OWNER

The Leo human loves to be needed and will undoubtedly dote all over his beloved touchy-feely, moody four-legged friend. Should the Leo human want someone he can tout around and look impressive with, an issue might arise, because the Cancer dog scoffs at such shameless self-promotion. But the Cancer doggie is devoted and will probably put up with these displays just to please his master. But keep in mind, Leo human, that the Cancer pooch needs way more attention and quality time at home than your socialite schedule may allow. Make extra time to spoil your sensitive pup in between red-carpet appearances and Cancer dog might stop whining for a few hours.

A CANCER DOG WITH A VIRGO OWNER

The Virgo human's fastidious nature bodes well for giving the needy Cancer doggie consistent attention and dependable TLC. The Virgo human is also more likely to use all-natural products and serve healthy dog food, making the Cancer pup pleased as punch. The two of you enjoy the simple pleasure of being together, whether it's lounging around in the park or grocery shopping or even a trip to the Laundromat. Chores are very satisfying to both of you and more fun when tackled together.

A Cancer Dog with a Libra Owner

The homebound Cancer pooch doesn't understand Libra's flirtatious flitting about town; with social Libra holding the leash, this moody pooch will have more walks than he can handle. The Cancer doggie might wonder, Why do we need to meet new people when I'm happy cuddling on the couch with you? Don't I give you enough licks? The Libra human is a social creature by nature, scoping out new clothes and admirers. She may have to coax her crib-loving Cancer poochie to change his reclusive ways. The Cancer doggie's moodiness could drive Libra to spend thousands on spa treatments just to decompress from the cantankerous household. Cancer will growl and pitch a fit just to embarrass graceful Libra at the most inopportune moments. The Cancer doggie loves that the Libra human keeps a peaceful and beautiful atmosphere at home, but going out is a whole other ball of wax.

A Cancer Dog with a Scorpio Owner

This pair is a human-dog psychic hotline. You don't have to speak when you can rely on telepathic communication. Scorpio will treat the Cancer dog with the highest level of devotion and the Cancer dog will be enamored of Scorpio human, dark side and all. You're such kindred souls, other doggies will get jealous of your intense bond. The Scorpio human knows intuitively what the Cancer doggie needs and will go to the ends of the earth to make sure the Cancer doggie feels safe and loved. Cancer doggie knows instinctually what Scorpio human needs and is always there in times of sickness and distress to mother and comfort Scorpio human. No one and nothing can come between these two soul mates.

A CANCER DOG WITH A SAGITTARIUS OWNER

The Sag loves planes; the Cancer loves the dog carrier to stay in one place—at home. A Sag human's need for constant movement might upset the sensitive Cancer doggie's constitution. If only the Sagittarius could compromise and read books about traveling, then the Cancer pup could provide some stability, a landing pad for the next adventure. The Cancer needs to know he's loved and appreciated and has an owner who's dependable; the free-floating Sag will have to learn to settle down and tend to the doggie dish as his first priority. While it's true that the two of you are like oil and water, the truth is that you will change each other's lives for the better.

A CANCER DOG WITH A CAPRICORN OWNER

The stoic Capricorn human will expect the Cancer pup to sleep on a bed of nails, metaphorically or otherwise. The Cancer will insist on sleeping in Capricorn's bed. You'll get nothing but silence from this baby of the zodiac until you realize that babying is all this poochie wanted in the first place. The Capricorn human prefers a reserved dog who can pretty much fend for himself, especially since the Capricorn often likes to work long hours—and the Cancer doggie is content to just stay home and eat and sleep for long stretches at a time. The Cancer doggie finds the Capricorn human's integrity very comforting. The Capricorn human can appreciate some of the crazier behaviors of the Cancer dog, because they both share a great and sarcastic sense of humor. As long as the Cancer dog learns to hold his own, Capricorn human might put down the ruler.

✳

A CANCER DOG WITH AN AQUARIUS OWNER

The unconventional Aquarius human might seem too wacko for the domestic Cancer pup. He's always bringing weird people over with loud voices and louder hairdos. The Aquarius wants to start a revolution; the Cancer just wants to redecorate the living room. If they can both learn that charity starts at home, this duo has real potential. The detached and aloof qualities of the Aquarius human could sometimes make the Cancer doggie feel unwanted, and the neediness of the Cancer doggie could make the Aquarian human feel resentful. But in the end the Cancer dog becomes more detached and the Aquarian more nurturing so the serious healing potential is worth a little bit of initial adjustment. Both are quirky and march to the beat of their own drummers but this match is more like a battle of the bands or a bittersweet symphony.

A CANCER DOG WITH A PISCES OWNER

This is so sweetly suitable for both sensitive watery types. You love all the same things in life—especially avoiding large crowds and sleeping as much as possible. After a while, the two of you start to feel like one. Hopefully you have a backyard so little effort needs to be exerted in terms of things like walking. Both could get lost for hours in a good movie or listening to classical music. You bring out the best in each other and can't imagine how you ever lived without each other for one single day.

TYPICAL CANCER BREEDS

✳

Great Dane, Cavalier King Charles Spaniel, Scottish Terrier

STAR SIGHTING: ACE—GREAT DANE

Most of us know this goofy and gentle giant as Scooby-Doo—but the Great Dane is also known as "the Apollo of all dogs." Word on the streets of Athens is that a very similar-looking dog was carved into a Greek coin dating back to 36 B.C. This handsome dog could go as far back as ancient Greece, though it was the Germans who admired this super creature so much that they began to breed these giant dogs.

Like an ideal mother, the Great Dane is a tender, sensitive, loving, caring, affectionate, noble, and dependable dog who loves his family more than anything else in the world. This giant is usually nice to people and other pets; however, he may appear aloof with a calm disposition. This is due to early training because of his size—an owner has to teach him early on to not lean on people or knock anyone or anything over.

In spite of his towering physique, a Great Dane can tolerate apartment living because he is pretty calm indoors and seems to enjoy being a homebody like a Cancer. However, he will require at least one long, romantic walk daily with a human.

REAL-LIFE EXAMPLES OF GREAT DANE/ CANCER TRAITS

- Ace is only three months old and is sophisticated enough to chew on *The Castle* by the legendary Cancerian writer, Franz Kafka (see photo).
- No puppy can be calmer than Ace; he's the perfect pup star!

DOG STAR *Leo*

(J u l y   2 3 – A u g u s t   2 2)

THE LEO DOG

ELEMENT: Fire

MODALITY: Fixed

RULERSHIP: Sun

SYMBOL: Lion

MOST COMPATIBLE WITH: Aries, Sagittarius, Gemini, Libra

WHAT A LEO DOG DAYDREAMS About: starring in their own movie; being chased by the paparazzi; starting their own doggie clothing line; performing in front of a sold-out crowd at Madison Square Garden

KEYWORDS: confident, show-off, proud, star quality, openhearted, generous, larger than life, dramatic, bold, bossy

THE LEO DOG STAR'S PERSONALITY

♌ The Leo dog needs an audience.

♌ The Leo dog lives for the limelight.

♌ The Leo dog loves affection, attention, praise, and a big fan club.

♌ The Leo dog needs to live a five-star lifestyle like the royalty she is.

♌ The Leo dog needs to be adored.

♌ The Leo dog needs to rule your world.

STAR SIGN CHARACTERISTICS

STRIKE A POSE

This is the super dog star of the zodiac: and don't you forget it! The Leo dog likes to strut like the little diva dog she is. She'll knock your socks off, whether she's performing or just looking as regal and mega-sophisticated as the Sphinx. Notice how she sits with unmatched elegance. The Leo Dog Star is the biggest show-off of the zodiac. A natural ham, she never gets enough time in the spotlight. The best way to feed her puffed-up pride is by showering her with compliments, attention, affection, and praise; and she'll take second helpings on that. She can never get enough: it's better than all the Greenies and liver snacks put together. Treat her like Hollywood royalty, lavish her in luxury items, five-star accommodations, and adorn her from head to toe in diamonds. Leo is the true show dog of the zodiac and the world is her audience. She'll sashay down the sidewalk like a supermodel whether it's an official contest or not. She's fabulous with children because she loves to play. But don't expect her to graciously share the limelight with the kids. She needs to be the center of attention twenty-four/seven, baby. She'll slobber you with kisses and wags galore because this A-list dog has a heart of gold.

I Am Dog, Hear Me Bark

The Leo Dog Star commands respect—if not an altar—upon which you vow to fervently worship her like the deity she is. Should you fail to pay her the proper respect, don't be surprised if she deals you some serious shade. Leo has a lot of pride to protect; she bruises as easily as she shines. If you neglect to pay attention to your Leo star—or worse yet, ignore her when she's showing off for you, it's like you've stolen the sunshine. This spoiled pup thrives on your adoration and affection; there's no such thing as too much. She has a heart of gold and would give you her last bone to prove her undying devotion.

The Leo diva wants only the best. She'll have no qualms telling you if she finds the surroundings beneath her high standards. Should you feed her measly canned food instead of cooking her a filet mignon, she'll throw a serious tantrum. Would you treat a royal Dog Star like that?

Dogs on Film

Don't hesitate to play paparazzi with your little show-off pooch. She is instantly insulted if you fail to have a revolving gallery of photos of her. She'd also appreciate it if you would keep a daily blog devoted to your obsession with her. While you're at it, be sure to deck your walls with her image—the bigger and more prominently displayed, the better. (Or you could just build a marquee and put her name in lights.) Don't hesitate to take as much video footage of your superstar as you possibly can. She is just so photogenic and natural on film—she was born for the big screen and large audiences. She loves nothing better on a Friday night than for you to fill your living room to maximum audience capacity and have a Leo Dog Star marathon of home movies starring yours truly plus an encore performance of stupid pet tricks. Don't hesitate to brag about her for hours or you'll hurt her pride. Get her an agent as early as possible: Leo is born for the big time.

IF THE LEO DOG COULD TALK

Don't you know who I am?

I oughta be in pictures!

Get my agent on the phone!

Look at the way I prance!

Brush me! I said, Brush me!

I'm the bomb!

Where's my servant? Oh, there you are, Mommy!

Where are you showing me off today?

Oh yes, that diamond necklace would look so pawfect on moi.

Let's have a ball, gourmet treats on ME!

When you got it, wag it!

I'm ready for my close-up.

WHAT A LEO DOG WANTS IN AN OWNER

J'ADORE

Requirement number one: You're into pet worship. Requirement number two: You like to live luxe. Requirement number three: The world revolves around *moi*. And that's just for starters. I need someone who is part owner/part agent/part fan club. You know how to hook me up with a personal chef, my own private dressing room, plush dog bed, fabulous wardrobe, and glamorous beauty products. You'll take the time to get to know what my favorites are and always have them on hand: like my favorite doggie shampoo, treats, and toys. If you're a cheapie or a tightwad, you'll offend my sensibilities. I need you to understand that I have champagne taste; a beer bottle budget won't cut it. We're *so* not happening. If your idea of fashion is some rag you bought from Wal-Mart, please don't expect me to be seen with you in public. I'd rather die. Okay, so I'm a bit of a drama queen: but you love that about me. I need an owner who has a, let's say, theatrical sensibility.

✳

If you take me out to the theater or own a theater yourself, even better. If you're famous: even better. If you're rich and famous: better, better, better! My doggie grooming bills rack up fast because a superstar must always look drop-dead gorgeous for her public.

WHERE'S MY AGENT?

If it's not obscenely obvious by now, I need to be spoiled, doted-on, catered-to, pampered, worshipped; in short: the sole purpose of your existence. Do you have what it takes to make me your all and everything? Are you fabulous enough (but not too fabulous; there's only room for one diva in this household)? Be sure to have plenty of photos of me in your phone, in your wallet, on your clothing. You may feel more like a PR agent than my owner, but what could be more glam, darling? There's never a lackluster moment with this superstar Dog Star. I know how to please the crowds and garner a fan club faster than you can say woof!

HOW TO EARN BROWNIE POINTS
FROM A LEO DOGGIE

Gourmet food	20 pts
Expensive accessories	20 pts
High-end fashion	20 pts
Doggie worship	20 pts
Five-star lifestyle	20 pts
	100 pts

COMPATIBILITY GUIDE

Most Compatible with: Aries, Sagittarius, Gemini, Libra

A LEO DOG WITH AN ARIES OWNER

This pair blows away the competition. The Aries human needs admiration and respect as much as the Leo dog. Both are born leaders but might wrestle for the leading role. An Aries human is often too independent to worship a Leo dog in the proper fashion. The Leo dog wishes the Aries human had better taste in clothes. They strengthen each other's already strong will and bravado: This is the little combo that could. Grammy's and Oscars adorn the mantelpiece.

A LEO DOG WITH A TAURUS OWNER

The Taurus human drives the Leo doggie nuts with her practical, penny-pinching ways. What about the five-star hotel, the diamond-studded collar? But when the Taurus human refuses to share food with the Leo doggie, the war is on. The Taurus human cannot believe one small furry animal could require such high maintenance. The Leo dog cannot believe one human could be such a snore. But deep down you're both such rock stars and have the kind of unmatched loyalty that truly makes for a long-lasting union. As long as you're into tug-of-wars and popularity contests, enjoy the rocky road, kids.

A LEO DOG WITH A GEMINI OWNER

The Leo dog will be *très* impressed with the Gemini hipster's trend-setting ways and jam-packed social calendar. The Gemini human has so many friends that

✳

the Leo is guaranteed a daily audience. A Gemini has no problem treating Leo like royalty, because Geminis are so easy and adaptable like that. A Leo dog keeps a Gemini human entertained for hours; the Gemini human always has a story to tell that will satisfy the Leo's sense of drama. Together, you're like Starsky and Hutch.

A LEO DOG WITH A CANCER OWNER

A Leo wants attention and so does a Cancer; but the Leo wants it from everyone and the Cancer human can't stand the paparazzilike crowds this doggie thrives on. The Leo wants out when the Cancer wants to stay in. A Leo will bark an a cappella Dog Star musical complete with a tap-dance number when a Cancer wants peace and quiet. If the Leo doggie can stand to be out of the spotlight for a minute then this match might have a chance; otherwise, the Cancer will pout until the Leo remembers that it's even more fun to spoil their best friend than to bask in more adoration from strangers.

A LEO DOG WITH A LEO OWNER

If they manage to stop fighting over the limelight for two seconds these two might realize all of the star-studded bonuses to their regal match. They'll know exactly how to flatter each other; a Leo dog knows how to pick up admirers for the Leo human, and together they could have their own show—starring: Okay, so they'll have to take turns, but it's worth all the extra attention. They are bona fide chick and dude magnets. People will line up to take your picture and get a kiss and a lick.

A LEO DOG WITH A VIRGO OWNER

The Virgo human will have to get used to Leo's flair for the dramatic. A Virgo likes things neat and simple; a Leo will make a mess just to get noticed. When this team goes out, both will have to look perfectly put together; but the Virgo doesn't mind being behind the scenes. They both need to live luxuriously; there's no end to the love between them as long as the Leo doggie can perform for someone else on occasion, so the Virgo can have some hermit time. But the Leo dog adores the way the Virgo human waits hand and foot on baby Leo dog.

A LEO DOG WITH A LIBRA OWNER

The Libra thinks the Leo pup is beautiful and tells her so—often. The Leo doggie understands Libra's need for beauty and balance; this goes hand and paw with Leo's grooming regimen, singing (make that howling) lessons, and gourmet doggie treats—and online fan club courtesy of Dogster. The Libra will take lots of pictures of her diva Dog Star. The Leo will return the favor with a flourish of licks, and doggie show tune renditions.

A LEO DOG WITH A SCORPIO OWNER

There have been better ideas in the history of dog-human relations, but differences aside, this makes a dynamic, intense little combo. A Scorpio is just the human to worship the Leo dog and vice versa; a Leo will fit right in with Scorpio's love of extremes. They're both passionate, dramatic, and will attract plenty of attention, which the Leo dog will lap up faster than you can say "Action!" However, the Scorpio will feel a little burned out if the Leo insists on hogging the spotlight for too long. Then again, it gives the Scorpio human the perfect excuse to go incognito. But if this prima donna dog pushes too hard, Scorpio may have no recourse but locking him up in the closet until he barks "mercy."

A Leo Dog with a Sagittarius Owner

The Sag human knows what makes this little dog tick. Applause, applause, applause—and some adventure and dramatic self-portraits thrown in the mix. With a Sag in the driver's seat, the Leo dog will have the wind in its fur, the sun on its back, and the rush of the open road. It's a good life. A Leo loves the Sag human's vivacious ways and loves meeting all of his jet-setting friends. As long as Leo gets to stand still long enough to strike a pose or two and let the admirers catch a few glimpses, this pup will truly feel like a megastar.

A Leo Dog with a Capricorn Owner

VIP meets star of the doggie zodiac when these two ladder-climbers get together. A Capricorn can manage the Leo dog's blossoming performance career; the Leo can remind the Capricorn human to have some fun, kick back, and enjoy the wealth. The Capricorn will be sure to buy Leo all of the latest doggie fashions—including silk scarves and high-end collars. The Capricorn human just needs to pencil in regular worshipping sessions. The issue is when the credit card bill comes and Capricorn human realizes he spent a freaking fortune on this demanding diva dog. Deprivation and punishment might be in order and there is bound to be some fur flying when Leo dog hears the word *no*.

Leo

A LEO DOG WITH AN AQUARIUS OWNER

The Aquarius has plenty of friends to feed a Leo dog's constant desire for adoration, but this little Dog Star might not get what he needs from an Aquarius human. Opposites might attract but they also create domestic spats. The Aquarius is too busy checking out the latest gadgets or reinventing the wheel to remember that the Leo needs an audience—*all the time*. They both love going out and having fun, but Leo's style is polished while Aquarius is wacky; in fact, the Leo dog might even be embarrassed to be seen with this goofball human—until he realizes that the Aquarius is always tuned into the next big thing.

A LEO DOG WITH A PISCES OWNER

Both Leo and Pisces live in la-la land. The Leo thinks the world revolves around her, and Pisces thinks the world doesn't even exist. Both dream of spending their days doing nothing but lounging around being pampered. The Pisces is sensitive to the Leo dog's high-maintenance M.O., and the Leo dog will be generously affectionate when the Pisces gets moody. When they go out for walks, the Pisces will just put on the shades and let the Leo have *all* the attention.

TYPICAL LEO BREEDS

Shih Tzu, Bichon Frise, and Pekingese

STAR SIGHTING: LOLA—SHIH TZU

This little lion is a doggie superstar! Originating from the Forbidden City of Beijing, the shih tzu was the Chinese royal family's favorite companion. This little princess will demand nothing but the best of everything from her servant—i.e., *you*. In return, you'll receive a trophy—i.e., the shih tzu—as well as unlimited kisses, love, joy, warmth, smiles, and entertainment.

Like a Leo, the shih tzu is packed with personality. She'll attract everyone on the street. If you're an introverted type who'd rather keep a low profile, think again before you choose a shih tzu. Walking around with this little drama queen will be equivalent to taking a walk with Madonna: greeting (or dodging) fans will

become part of your lifestyle. This popular little glamour dog is a shiny, happy, playful dog that is also clever, alert, dignified, courageous, and proud.

Shih tzus play well with gentle and considerate children and are generally friendly with other dogs as long as they don't try to steal the limelight. They can be a little stubborn and may require consistent and patient training to be housebroken. They are great apartment dogs, but make sure you have a good air-conditioning system for the hot summers. Shih tzus have a royal sense of entitlement, which may become overwhelming for some; but most will be smitten by their lavish displays of charm and grandiosity.

REAL-LIFE EXAMPLES OF SHIH TZU/LEO TRAITS

- Lola's mom is a dancer and often brings her along to dance workshops. Whenever the dancers form a circle, Lola runs around in the center, demanding applause.
- Lola entered her first doggie fashion show contest at her local nursing home; she received so much attention—from the seniors to the medical staff—that she's hooked on competitions.

✳

DOG STAR
Virgo

6

(August 23 – September 22)

THE VIRGO DOG

ELEMENT: Earth

MODALITY: Mutable

RULERSHIP: Mercury

SYMBOL: Virgin

MOST COMPATIBLE WITH: Taurus, Capricorn, Scorpio, and Cancer

WHAT A VIRGO DOG DAYDREAMS ABOUT: neat, ordered rows of healthy dog food; a house that never has a spot of dirt

KEYWORDS: neat, meticulous, worrywart tendencies, fastidious, healthy, minimalist, hermitlike, hard working

THE VIRGO DOG STAR'S PERSONALITY

♍ The Virgo dog needs a clean dog dish.

♍ The Virgo dog wants the vitamin supplements.

♍ The Virgo dog loves a minimalist environment to keep his mind uncluttered.

♍ The Virgo dog wants a simple life.

♍ The Virgo dog loves order and routine.

♍ The Virgo dog likes things pristine.

♍ The Virgo dog worries when things get chaotic.

STAR SIGN CHARACTERISTICS

MR. CLEAN

Picky? Why, yes! Fussy? But of course! Smart as a whip? You know it. The epitome of perfection in the canine species, the Virgo Dog Star reigns supreme of the clean and pristine. You'll have to keep an eye on his nervous nature and worrywart tendencies, especially if the home lacks order or the owner lacks good hygiene. This dog loves ritual. Seriously, you'll have to set your alarm clock like you're in military boot camp for waking and walking and feeding times. The conscientious Virgo will keep you on track, too. If you're the type who spends five minutes running around like mad looking for your keys or always goes out wearing two different-colored socks, you'll be reformed by this disciplined doggie. He doesn't miss a detail. If you forget about an important meeting, a Virgo will be sure to point it out on your calendar with his well-groomed paws.

SHHHHH! SILENCE IS GOLDEN

You might be surprised to encounter such a thoughtful dog who, unlike his Mercury-ruled friend Gemini, would bark nonstop all 365 days of the year if he could. A Virgo dog relishes their quiet time and solitude (as long as they know you are nearby). He thinks deeply and frequently, often trying to assimilate and organize their experience. A Virgo wants to know the meaning behind everything and will take things apart (as long as it doesn't make too much of a mess) to figure it all out. Don't be surprised if your Virgo pooch gets a furrowed furry brow from all of that analyzing and worrying. If he watches television with you, don't insult him with mindless sitcoms or trashy cable shows. He appreciates the news, thoughtful political commentary, and artfully made documentaries. Remember, he has high standards in all arenas of life. Do not, we pray, do not underestimate this pooch's brilliance.

HOW MUCH IS THAT DOGGIE IN THE HABIT?

You'll wonder if this dog wasn't intended to be a monk but was born into the wrong species. The Virgo Dog Star was born to serve his master and ultimately, the world. If he were human, he would be a nurse, a healer, or your most loyal servant. A Virgo wants to be clean and healthy—and they want you to clean up your act, too. This Dog Star can inspire you to kick your bad habits and keep your house spic and span. This puppy won't need as much obedience school or dog training as most dogs: He's born with an innate ability to avoid the uncouth behaviors typically associated with sloppier stars. Jumping up on people and ruining their white clothing with doggie paw prints?! No way. The thought of slobber and mud and matted hair makes him cringe. Being such a smarty-pants, however, he may be too intelligent to train with simple obedience school. He may shun anything inferior to his own superior manners. A Virgo can and will inspire you to be the model parent of perfect breeding to match his own unparalleled levels of perfection. Of course with his godlike unconditional love, he'll forgive you for being merely human.

IF THE VIRGO DOG COULD TALK

Perfection, please!

Hey, you missed a spot there when cleaning my doggie bowl.

Eeew . . . when was the last time you washed my dog bed?

Excuse me, I'm trying to get some beauty sleep . . . would you stop talking, please?

Rise and shine! Wake up! I'm ready to start my day!

How about some classical music this time?

The heavy metal is giving me a headache.

Is he crazy not buying me any supplements to take with this junky dog food?

Does she really think I'm going to wear that tacky sweater?

Where are my doggie paw wipes?

Hey, I don't want love handles like yours, you better take me for a run or

I'll stand in front of this damn TV all night.

WHAT A VIRGO DOG WANTS IN AN OWNER

THE TAO OF HUMAN

I need someone who appreciates Zen-like minimalism—or a classic elegance in the home environment. Too much clutter makes me nervous. I will worry away hours planning better organizational strategies. You'll get extra doggie points if you're fanatical about your hygiene. "Cleanliness is next to godliness" is my mantra. I just adore an owner who understands the importance of bathing a few times a day. Dirt, grime, and germs can send me over the edge. I need a pristine place to call home. I need an owner who knows the value of spending a little extra for nutritious dog food. If you think Purina is going to fly, think again. I can sniff out an artificial ingredient from a mile away. I am fussy with a capital F! Daily exercise is the most important of all: no flab for the fab, I say. You have to live up to my high standards. I'm no schlep of a mutt, mind you. Ne'er-do-well's need not apply.

YOU WORK HARD FOR THE MONEY

It makes me smile from ear to ear whenever I see you hard at work, honing your craft. I love nothing more than someone who believes practice makes perfect. It gives me a sense of peacefulness and reassurance just knowing that you're attending to all of the details with so much love and care (especially when those details involve moi). It makes it feel like all is well and right in my doggie world. When I see you getting better at your talents as a result of practice, I am so proud of you. I also hope you will help me refine my skills like fetching and catching and standing on two legs and spinning. The more time you take with me to help me perfect my talents the more it will be appreciated. I love hard work and feeling like I am as close to perfect as possible.

RETREAT ME

Quiet time is oh-so-necessary to keep my fur on straight. I can easily get frazzled with too much on my mind, so a nice quiet meditation room at home with my doggie bed in it would be mucho appreciated. If you're a quiet type yourself, all the better to keep me from feeling high-strung. Humble types prevent me from compulsive fur licking and tail chewing. My dream owner would be a monk or a total ascetic personality, or at least an OCD type who insists on perfectly white linens everywhere including on my doggie lounge chair. I love a streamlined pad to call my home. The more perfectly defined nooks and crannies to keep out the clutter, the better! This way we can both keep our thoughts clear—and more important, our schedules clear, allowing ample time to practice my new tricks. Practice makes perfect.

HOW TO EARN BROWNIE POINTS
FROM A VIRGO DOGGIE

Healthy treats	20 pts
Clean dog bowl and bed	20 pts
Lots of exercise	20 pts
Clean and neat home	20 pts
Stick to a routine	20 pts
	100 pts

COMPATIBILITY GUIDE

Most Compatible with: Taurus, Capricorn, Scorpio, Cancer

A VIRGO DOG WITH AN ARIES OWNER

The Virgo dog might find the Aries human a bit too loud and bold for his nervous temperament. He might also feel a bit smothered by the overexuberant, protective Aries human. The Aries human doesn't understand the Virgo's need to meditate. Why would anyone, let alone a dog, need so much quiet time? But the Virgo dog will appreciate the long runs in the park and the chance to put his reform skills into action. If the Aries can find his quiet side and learn to burn off some energy in a serious cleaning fit, then this combo could work like a well-oiled machine rather than as an Oscar and Felix.

✳

A VIRGO DOG WITH A TAURUS OWNER

Excellent match. Both Virgo and Taurus are earth signs and like things solid. The Virgo dog appreciates the Taurean love of beauty and fine taste. If the human has a classic Taurus garden, even more gold doggie stars—and licks—will be rewarded. A Taurus loves steady routine, which will please the Virgo doggie's need for ritual. Potential clash: The Virgo dog could find the Taurus human a bit too stubborn and bossy. Also, the "bull in the china shop" or hedonistic type of Taurus will not go over well with a Virgo. If the Taurus learns to practice refinement, this could make a fabulous relationship.

A VIRGO DOG WITH A GEMINI OWNER

If the Gemini human is a typical jabber-jaw, she might give the nervous Virgo a case of doggie hypertension. A Virgo needs peace and quiet; incessant cell phone gab could drive this poor pooch over the edge. Mercury rules both, so the Virgo will appreciate the Gemini human's curious nature and analytical mind. The Virgo pooch will be entertained for hours by their detailed and dramatic stories; the Gemini will never lack someone to talk to. Just remember to *fermez la bouche* when it's bedtime.

A VIRGO DOG WITH A CANCER OWNER

Both dog and human love to hide out at home. The Cancer will give her pup plenty of nurturing, which the Virgo will appreciate and return. Being such a natural culinary expert, the Cancer human will be inspired to whip up fancy and nutritious meals for her beloved Virgo pup. The Cancer is a born mommy or daddy anyway, so of course she won't forget the Virgo's daily vitamin supplements.

A Virgo Dog with a Leo Owner

Depending on how flashy the Leo human is, this glamorous duo is destined for a run in Vegas; or for the more upscale and sophisticated types, they might be the stars of many an independent artsy film. The Virgo craves quality over flash; the Leo's luxurious tastes will please this pooch to no end. Leos are also known for their generosity—what dog wouldn't lap that all up? Just remember: The Virgo pup needs to be showered with gifts from the grooming gods and the doggie health food store.

A Virgo Dog with a Virgo Owner

Soul mates, or a recipe for an OCD disaster? Does this pair feed each other's neuroses or quell them? If their shared neurotic tendencies create more anxiety than peace of mind, they'll have to trade the caffeine routine for some chamomile tea. The good news is that the Virgo dog's need for order will ease the human's worried mind considerably: Even if he goes for a roll in the mud, he'll magically come out looking clean. But someone better take some valium or at least some kava kava before the Swiffer turns into a weapon.

A Virgo Dog with a Libra Owner

Both dog and human have exquisite taste; both hate nothing more than tackiness. Both love things clean and simple; the Libra human's balanced ways will calm a nervous Virgo dog from the first instant. The Libra is always looking out for the needs of others, so the Virgo pooch will feel well attended to. They'll find kinship in their taste for beautiful things like Monet and Browning.

A Virgo Dog with a Scorpio Owner

The Virgo pup adores the Scorpio's intelligence and quiet intensity. Both are fiercely loyal and share a connection that goes beyond words and the general dog-human interactions. The Scorpio human keeps the perfect low-light ambiance to quell Virgo's nervous system; the Virgo's sheer presence reminds Scorpio to tackle that clutter in the back of the closet and under the bed.

A Virgo Dog with a Sagittarius Owner

These two mix about as well as oil and water. A Sag needs a pooch with more spontaneity than a Virgo dog provides; the Virgo will want to scream: "Simmer down now, crazy human!" The Sag is too peppy; the Virgo needs calm. A Sag doesn't have the time or patience to stress over the details of a Virgo's basic needs. The Virgo pup's beloved quiet time goes right out the window along with the vitamins and the dog brush. The only time they meet each other eye to eye is when the Virgo needs to burn off some nervous energy. But traveling to Singapore is not exactly the Virgo's idea of relaxation or positive remedial action. Plus, if the Sag human trips over the dog one more time, the pooch is bound to develop an ulcer.

A Virgo Dog with a Capricorn Owner

A Virgo dog won't find anything to nitpick with this upstanding human. A Capricorn is all about the high end and a Virgo is the bona fide high-end pooch. The Capricorn human will score points with her wise and sophisticated ways; the Virgo doggie will lap up the luxury that the Capricorn has worked her whole life to provide. Together, they're sure to be the envy of Madison Avenue and Rodeo Drive.

A VIRGO DOG WITH AN AQUARIUS OWNER

Both dog and human are so eccentric and on such different paths in life that it would require an act of fate or a pushy pet store employee to bring this pair together. Both are quirky and prone to anxiety, so relaxing together is a pipedream. But a few days with a Virgo dog will give the Aquarius human more focus and efficiency than ever before; the Virgo dog may even learn to like strange groups of people.

A VIRGO DOG WITH A PISCES OWNER

Unless they're one of those rare Pisces humans who stress the details, this could be messy. If they're the typical escapist Pisces who likes to spend the majority of life horizontal, then the mostly vertical Virgo pooch might feel like he's drowning in an ocean of neglect. Trying to calm the pup's nerves with a shot of brandy will only make things worse. Art therapy is recommended for this pair: the Virgo dog will appreciate Piscean disorder if it's beautiful. Try painting, reading poetry, listening to sonatas—this satisfies the Pisces' need for escapism and the Virgo's nerves will be soothed.

TYPICAL VIRGO BREEDS

Weimaraner, Dalmatian, and Hungarian Vizsla

STAR SIGHTING: FRANZ— WEIMARANER

A Weimaraner can roll around in mud and come out looking squeaky clean and handsome: now *that's* a typical Virgo trait. This dog is more than just its looks: It's got a whole lot of grace and attitude, and a personality that screams perfection! It's hard to find a dog as versatile as a Weimie, with its friendly nature, loyalty, tireless energy, fearlessness, alertness, speed, stamina, and superb level of intelligence.

Weimies were originally bred for hunting but these smarty-pants will learn to adapt to your lifestyle quickly. Rules and directions must be established early on or they can easily outsmart you. You need to let your Weimie pup know who's in charge or you'll most likely experience some major power struggles down the road. Friendly under most circumstances, they're also extremely devoted to their

family and can be protective; it would be wise to socialize your Weimie with friends and other pups early on.

REAL-LIFE EXAMPLES OF WEIMERANER/ VIRGO TRAITS

- Franz has a daddy who loves to hide out in his study and read all day; of course, he wants to keep him company but cannot stand the chaos and mess in the room. Franz only goes into the study when it's clean and organized.
- Franz would only drink tap water if he were dying from thirst; he prefers natural spring water but ice-cold Brita will do. His favorite treat is carrots.
- When he's taken to sidewalk cafes, Franz will stand the whole time if there isn't a towel on the ground for him to lie on.

7

DOG STAR *Libra*

(S e p t e m b e r   2 3 – O c t o b e r   2 2)

THE LIBRA DOG

ELEMENT: Air

MODALITY: Cardinal

RULERSHIP: Venus

SYMBOL: Scales

MOST COMPATIBLE WITH: Gemini, Aquarius, Leo, and Sagittarius

WHAT A LIBRA DOG DAYDREAMS ABOUT: peace on earth; a life of luxury

KEYWORDS: balanced, calm, peaceful, beautiful, sweet, accommodating, fair-minded, charming, social

THE LIBRA DOG STAR'S PERSONALITY

♎ The Libra dog loves to have an equal partner to do everything with.

♎ The Libra dog has an innate sense of fair play.

♎ The Libra dog loves all things beautiful.

♎ The Libra dog needs the scales to be perfectly balanced.

♎ The Libra dog needs social events with beautiful pooches and people.

♎ The Libra dog needs peace at any price.

♎ The Libra dog is all sweetness and light.

♎ The Libra dog needs attention.

♎ The Libra dog needs to please others.

♎ The Libra dog needs charm.

STAR SIGN CHARACTERISTICS

MIGHTY DOG MEETS APHRODITE

With so much discord in the world, who couldn't use some beauty and harmony? Thank heavens for the charming and gracious ways of a little Libran pup to bring everything back into perfect equanimity and equipoise. Libran pooches are the peacemakers of the zodiac, blessed with an innate sense of balance. You'll rarely see your Libran darling display any unpleasant or extreme behaviors. Gentle as a lamb and gorgeous as a supermodel, it's as if she were born with a perfect pedigree and manners to boot. The Libran's sole purpose is to charm and compliment you, her partner for life. She will do everything in her puppy powers to please and accommodate you. You will always come first, as Librans want nothing more than to please their other half. To them, life is one grand balancing act. Their mission is to keep everything flowing smoothly. They will always avoid the ugliness of extremes.

ALL YOU NEED IS LOVE

Librans abhor nothing more than confrontation and fighting. It completely throws them out of whack. You know the saying "War is harmful to children and other living things"? This goes double for your Libran pooch. She's ultrasensitive to conflict. A warlike home environment, discord, anger, and injustice will flip her scales, so it's advisable to do everything you can to keep the peace around the home front. If you're a more tempestuous type of human, she'll happily give you a course in anger management, letting it all just roll off your back. What's worth getting so worked up about? For Venus-ruled Libra, having peace of mind is the highest virtue. Why sweat the small stuff? Life is so beautiful, so enjoyable, and so harmonious when we all just get along and love each other. An easygoing Libran doggie will teach you how to kick the trifles and petty problems with her pretty little heels. Anger is so unbecoming. This little love goddess Dog Star knows that beauty and harmony have to rule.

WITH LIBERTY AND JUSTICE AND DOGGIE TREATS FOR ALL

Libran doggies can't stand seeing injustice. They'd weep over your morning *Times* if they knew how to read it. Don't try to hide it from them, though. They want to make the world a better place. You'll have to keep them informed, because they'll know intuitively when their Libran sense of fairness is needed. If she can get her paws on writings by Gandhi or MLK she'll beg you to read them to her at bedtime. This sweet little pup wants everyone to enjoy the good life. Watch your harmonious pup in action at the park. She'd never let another dog steal a toy or a bone from her friend. She won't fight, though—she'll use more evolved tactics, such as barking diplomatically or convincing a human to come to her aid. She'd make a wonderful lawyer for the underdog. Intensely loyal and devoted to justice, if your Libran Dog Star feels you are being treated unfairly, she'll immediately start barking a well-thought, balanced argument in your defense.

IF THE LIBRA DOG COULD TALK

Can you put some sugar on this kibble?

NO, what do YOU want to do?

Let me weigh my options.

I feel pretty, oh so pretty!

That's not fair!

Let's agree to disagree.

I want to go to the peace walk!

Can we volunteer at the homeless shelter?

It's a blessing in disguise . . . just let it go.

To each dog her own.

Bark and let bark.

WHAT A LIBRA DOG WANTS IN AN OWNER

THE PRETTY PARTNER

Tell me a thousand times a day that I'm pretty! I need you to want me to go everywhere with you. We're a team: two peas in a pod, two bugs in a rug, two halves that make a whole. I want to do everything with you! Everything's better when we're together, don't you agree?! Oh, how I love someone chill, someone who can really go with the flow: just like me. I can't stand people who sweat the small stuff. What's worth getting so stressed out about, anyway?

FAIR AND SQUARE

Okay, so I sometimes have a hard time making up my mind. I like a pleasantly decisive owner, as long as you choose well and fairly. I really need someone who understands how to keep things in perfect equilibrium. I will give you everything but please don't take advantage of my good nature. I can be a bit naïve and gullible but I'm no dummy. Don't underestimate my intelligence. I am a brilliant judge of character and will sense when you are treating me unfairly. I really need an owner who will do the "right" thing. If you try to skirt around the law or go against your conscience, it's going to affect my kidneys.

DOGGIE GOLIGHTLY

I love to be around people, where I can flirt and flirt, so if you're more of a wall-flower, this may not be a love connection for me. I prefer a socialite, especially someone on the A-list so they can show off my beauty to other beautiful people who will call me "gorgeous" all the time. So I'm a bit narcissistic; who isn't? I'm such a charmer: I'll have all of your friends and family wrapped around my little paw instantly. If you need to use me as a girl or boy magnet, I'm your dog! I attract people to me like bees to honey! If you don't charm them, I will!

HOW TO EARN BROWNIE POINTS
WITH A LIBRA DOGGIE

Sweets!	20 pts
Pretty accessories	20 pts
Peaceful and chic home	20 pts
Parties with beautiful dogs and humans	20 pts
Do charity work with her	20 pts
	100 pts

COMPATIBILITY GUIDE

✳

Most Compatible with: Gemini, Aquarius, Leo, Sagittarius

A Libra Dog with an Aries Owner

Yikes! An Aries may be way too independent for this partner-oriented pup. The Libran doggie will be devastated to be left at home while the Aries owner is off in hot pursuit of the next conquest. The short-fused Aries may throw off the Libra's delicate balance—especially if she likes to yell or scream when frustrated. At the slightest sign of discord, the conflict-weary Libran doggie will be horrified, whereas the Mars-ruled Aries loves nothing more than a good fight. But as history proves, Mars and Venus have learned to get along. The Aries might learn to appreciate the beautiful things in life, like smelling the flowers rather than plowing right through them; the Libran doggie could use some lessons in decision making and who better than the impulsive Aries to show them how it's done?

A Libra Dog with a Taurus Owner

Together they'll happily pursue a life of leisure, as they each bring out the other's lazier side. This peace-loving combo of sweetness and light loves days filled with shopping and gardening (and yes, you guessed it, food). A Libran dog can help a Taurus avert indulgent ruts and achieve greater equilibrium in life. The Taurus human helps the Libra pooch develop a firmer resolve.

A Libra Dog with a Gemini Owner

Being the two charmers of the zodiac, they'll undoubtedly collect bazillions of admirers. Always on their way to the next best scene, soon they'll notice they *are* the scenes themselves. If the Gemini human does the talking, the Libran dog can take care of the flirting. They make the ultimate partners in fun, and their social calendars are always jam-packed. Of course, no decision is ever firm and nothing is written in stone but they just call that keeping things flexible.

A Libra Dog with a Cancer Owner

Truth be told, there could be some *ish* (as in *issues*), darling. A-list Libran doggies hate being pent-up in the house when they could be out working their charm. Introverted and domestic Cancer may find herself in a quandary as to what to do with this social butterfly pup. They'll have to learn to strike a balance between quiet home time and scoping-out-other-dogs time. The Cancer human might dress the Libran dog in the ugliest dog sweater imaginable just to discourage social flitting. Libra doggie will not be happy with this ugly punishment. Ruff. Ruff.

A Libra Dog with a Leo Owner

This is love—make that worship—at first sight. The Leo owner will love the constant showering of licks and affection bestowed by an ultra-loving Libran doggie; the Libra enjoys being out on the town with the beautiful Leo. This is a power couple who will instantly take over the world and leave a trail of broken hearts in its wake. Expect an endless flow of stroking and cooing between dog and human and all of their many admirers.

A Libra Dog with a Virgo Owner

There's very little to fuss or fret about in this combination. And for a Virgo, that's saying something. A Libra dog is like instant therapy and a spa vacation wrapped into one. The Virgo human keeps everything so neatly organized that the Libra doggie never loses her balance. The Libra pup likes to fingerpaint in the tub but hates cleaning up; the Virgo doesn't appreciate the mess but does like the Libra's aesthetic sensibility.

A LIBRA DOG WITH A LIBRA OWNER

Is this match based on total harmony and bliss or are you both so covered in fairy dust that no one ever busts a move or makes up their mind? But then again, they'll both chime in: *Who cares! Decisions are so overrated!* As long as they've got plenty of beauty, art, love, and good food, all is right with the world. Life is one pretty parade with flowers and big hats. The sticky sweetness might make less nicey-nice types sick to their stomachs or charm the pants off the neighborhood depending on how they flaunt their loveliness.

A LIBRA DOG WITH A SCORPIO OWNER

Lovable Libra is the perfect little guru for the intense, brooding Scorpio. The darling Libran doggie has come to teach the Scorpio the beauty of avoiding extremes and maintaining a peaceful, harmonious state of mind. This pup will feed the Scorpio human instant calm, and all of that poise will start to rub off. With a Libra pooch around, the Scorpio human almost never gets into trouble—well, at least while his dog is watching. And the Scorpio thought he'd never learn to embrace his more angelic side! But truthfully, how long will the Scorpio human want to play nice? Eventually he will return to the dark side even if it means taking the pooch down with him. The underground is no place for Libran dogs.

✳

A Libra Dog with a Sagittarius Owner

Gregarious rainbow-chasers, both are forever seeking greener pastures. For these two, life is like an endless convertible ride on a sunny day listening to a Frank Sinatra recording. The Sag is decisive enough for both, so together they'll actually have a plan and follow it through to the end. A Libran dog is like medicine for the high-strung Sag human; a Sag is like a Libra's personal trainer and motivational speaker wrapped into one.

A Libra Dog with a Capricorn Owner

The Capricorn human might cramp Libra's style a little too much for comfort. All work and no play could make him a dull and disappointing owner for this peppy pup. A Libra wants to run and play and see people. That said, with this doggie by a Capricorn's side, the pragmatic Goat might learn to lighten up and appreciate the sweeter things in life: like daffodils and sunsets and nice long breaks from work. The Capricorn human might even leave the office early (on occasion) to spend time with this little cupcake of a pooch. Then again, probably not.

A Libra Dog with an Aquarius Owner

Best friends for life! These two are so well suited; they'll never stumble on the bumpy path of life. They bring out each other's best qualities, like friendship and fairness. Both dog and human are concerned with all of the social problems contributing to injustice in the world. Libra will be the poster dog of the peace campaign while the Aquarius human works diligently behind the scenes. Together they can bring the dreams of John and Yoko to life—world peace! Ruff! Ruff!

A LIBRA DOG WITH A PISCES OWNER

This pair is poetry in motion as they search for life's finer distractions together. Both would rather live in a fantasy world than the actual dismal or mundane world of reality. It's all smoke and mirrors and bliss for these two. The Libra dog will have to keep one paw firmly planted on the ground at all times, for she knows that she's the backbone in this relationship. When the Pisces human is asleep, the Libra pooch will have to step up and do the chores. The Pisces human can learn from the Libra doggie that there is hope in life as long as there is unconditional love.

TYPICAL LIBRA BREEDS

Labrador Retriever, Golden Retriever, and Poodle

STAR SIGHTING: FORTUNATE— LABRADOR RETRIEVER

The most popular breed on the North American continent, the Lab has earned her place in people's hearts by pleasing them to death. Like classic Libras, the Lab needs peace and harmony at all times and will do whatever it takes to avoid friction. In fact, the Lab can easily outdo Librans in the people-pleasing department: A Lab has no limits when it comes to making people happy. Even the poster

＊

Libra boy, Gandhi, didn't succeed in pleasing everyone; the Lab has got to be the winner!

Well-balanced, loving, affectionate, patient, loyal, intelligent, eager, reliable, and good-natured, Labs are by far the most-used breed for service dogs. They guide the blind and disabled and many are therapy dogs or serve on search-and-rescue teams. Originally bred in Newfoundland to be tough, icy-water dogs to help fishermen pull their nets to shore, Labs also have a rugged side that appeals to the tough guys with their hunting, tracking, and retrieving skills. They are also popular in the police force as narcotics detectors.

Labs can handle apartment living but they definitely need exercise. They are super friendly and excellent with children and other pets. Train them early on not to pull because they have strong necks. Thankfully, they are easy to train. They love food as much as Libra humans, so watch their weight!

REAL-LIFE EXAMPLES OF LABRADOR RETRIEVER/LIBRA TRAITS

- Fortunate was only 6 weeks old at the time of the photo shoot, but it was clear from her angelic little face that she was born to be a professional people pleaser.
- It's almost time for Fortunate's first birthday bash now and her proud mother confirms her people-pleasing tendencies. Fortunate walks right by her side, never ahead of her, like a true partner without ever being trained for that. A large-dog owner's dream!
- The words "conflict" or "fight" are not in Fortunate's vocabulary.

8

DOG STAR

Scorpio

(October 23 – November 21)

THE SCORPIO DOG

ELEMENT: Water

MODALITY: Fixed

RULERSHIP: Mars/Pluto

SYMBOL: Scorpion

MOST COMPATIBLE WITH: Cancer, Pisces, Virgo, and Capricorn

WHAT SCORPIO DOG DAYDREAMS ABOUT: Sharing all your deep, dark secrets late at night in the candlelight; helping you track down the clues of a cheating ex-lover

KEYWORDS: Intensity, control, passionate, extremes, secretive, suspicious, intelligent, devoted, sensitive, jealous

THE SCORPIO DOG STAR'S PERSONALITY

♏ The Scorpio dog demands loyalty.

♏ The Scorpio dog's motto is all or nothing.

♏ The Scorpio dog sees right through your every motive.

♏ The Scorpio dog wants all the dirt.

♏ The Scorpio dog needs you to go to hell and back to prove your love.

♏ The Scorpio dog needs lots of reassurance that you're eternally devoted.

♏ The Scorpio dog needs the intensity level turned up.

STAR SIGN CHARACTERISTICS

PUPPY POWER

Never underestimate the power of this mysterious canine. If you want a dog that would go to hell and back for you, this is the one. The Scorpio dog is shrewd, intense, and religiously devoted to those she deems worthy; and she expects nothing less from you. If you think that having the ability to stand on two legs means you can sneak anything past her: think again. The Scorpio will see right through you and by golly, you'll feel it. Fiercely possessive and beyond jealous, should you fail to show a Scorpio pup your undivided attention she may resort to giving you the silent treatment: or at least you'll feel a shortage of licks for a while. You'll have to prove your undying love and regain her trust.

Snoop Doggie Dog

This passionate pooch has a strong lust for life, but beware of the skeletons in her dog carrier. This magnetic pooch likes to live a little bit on the edge. Notice how she jumps into the street without looking or tries to pick fights with other dogs just to see what they're made of. Or maybe she sneaks people food or snoops in your closets when you're not at home. Whatever it is, she gets a thrill out of getting into whatever is off limits. The Scorpio is so sly, but you'd never guess it. She seems so innocent and angelic on the surface, how could such a sweetie pie ever do any harm? Play a game of rollover and you might find a little underbelly to your precious pup. See that sly grin, that devious look in the eyes? Look behind the couch: You'll probably find some hidden accoutrements that your dear one has snagged when you least expected it. This smarty-pants pup is also a sneaky Pete.

Self-Destructo Dog

It's true that all dogs are supposed to love you unconditionally—and that's all fine and good—but you'll have to take extra good care of this one. The supersensitive Scorpio doggie needs oodles of reassurance from you to feel truly loved. Her worst fear is that someday you'll take her for granted or grow lukewarm in your affection for her. This Dog Star is so passionate about everything that she feels it when you start to detach from her even the slightest bit. She may have no choice but to protect her feelings by becoming aloof and distant from you, too. Only a Scorpio dog could give you a bit of the cold shoulder or harbor any secret doggie fantasies of revenge when her feelings get hurt. In most cases, she would much rather be your little angel and show you how she would risk any danger to demonstrate her undying devotion for you. A Scorpio dog has the potential to be deeply wounded. Be forewarned: This dog has a fearless edge and likes to flirt with danger. Keep her on a tight leash should you notice any daredevil behaviors from this hardcore pooch.

IF THE SCORPIO DOG COULD TALK

What's she hiding under there?

You don't want to get on my bad side.

Don't get mad, get even.

Let's raise a little Cain.

Would you die for me?

I'll call your bluff.

It's her, or me; who's it going to be?

Don't mess with my mommy!

It's all or nothing!

An eye for an eye, a growl for a growl.

WHAT A SCORPIO DOG WANTS IN AN OWNER

DOG OR DIE

Would you die for me? Don't give me any flim-flam devotion: I want the kind of owner who would sacrifice everything for me. I'd give you nothing less in return. I'll forsake all others to worship the ground you walk on with religious fervor. If you're the type who gets all ga-ga with your dog or treats her in a condescending manner, then I ain't the one, honey. I hate baby talk. If you want to make me ill, raise your voice ten octaves and watch my fur crawl. Let's be straight: I am the *real deal,* not some superficial fluff ball you can butter up with compliments. If you don't say what you mean and mean what you say, you'll leave me no choice but to ignore you. Truth be told, I dig a sarcastic, sardonic wit in my owner. I want to know all your deep, dark secrets—you know, the ones that you haven't dared to share with anyone else.

AIN'T NO HALF-STEPPIN'

Please do your best to understand and appreciate my intensity. If you share in the same extreme likes and dislikes, we're going to get on famously. If you're one of those middle-ground, middle-path moderate types, it ain't gonna work, my friend. I don't do halfway, half-assed, half-hearted wishy-washy blasé blasé. And please, if you're the type who has to fawn over every four-legged furry friend that crosses your path, you'll drive me to an early grave. I'm sorry, but I'm just too doggone jealous to have to share your attention even for a second. Please don't torture me like that. It's all or nothing with me, kid.

✳

NIGHT FEVER

Oh, and how I would adore an owner who's pretty much a carbon copy of me: a nocturnal creature who isn't afraid of the dark. I want you to take me out prowling at night with you, to explore the hidden, the forbidden, the forsaken, leaving no stone unturned. But when I'm at home I need low light, shades down, and privacy plus. I prefer to sleep during the day and roam the night. Prepare yourself for some major resistance should you need to wake me up at the crack of dawn for one of those god-forsaken sunrise walks. Unless we've decided to keep an all-night vigil together, it's going to take some extra coaxing and some treats to turn me into such an early bird, darling.

DOGGIAN ANALYST

I'll let you in on a little secret (my favorite expression): I admire an owner who isn't afraid to delve into the depths of her psyche—nothing superficial but deep where the skeletons reside. Even if you refuse to do so, I won't. I need to know what really makes my owner tick. Oh yes, and please, please, please read me psychological thrillers or murder mysteries, it makes my fur crawl with delight. Either that or let's analyze our subconscious dreams and fears—just keep it deep with me. I was a psychologist in my past life and I still have the ability to read between the lines. In case you're wondering why I have this odd propensity to stare you down for hours on end, I'm simply analyzing your every move like a good little Freudian Dog Star. I have an extreme B.S. detector: I can tell if you're giving me the truth or lying to yourself. Keep it real with me and we'll be best buds for eternity.

HOW TO EARN BROWNIE POINTS
FROM A SCORPIO DOGGIE

Undivided attention	20 pts
Midnight walks	20 pts
Detective games	20 pts
Black leather leash and collar	20 pts
Privacy plus	20 pts
	100 pts

COMPATIBILITY GUIDE

Most Compatible with: Cancer, Pisces, Virgo, Capricorn

A SCORPIO DOG WITH AN ARIES OWNER

This is a high-energy dog-human combo. Both are fiercely passionate and strong-willed. As long as the Aries human doesn't get bossy and push the Scorpio dog around by telling him to walk faster and bark louder, this match is exceptional. If the Aries gets too domineering, the sensitive Scorpio doggie may just have to teach this dummy a lesson by recoiling in silence for a few years, leaving the Aries banging his head against the wall. The Aries blows off steam quickly, but the Scorpio neither forgives nor forgets.

✳

A SCORPIO DOG WITH A TAURUS OWNER

As long as control issues don't dominate the domestic scene and the Taurus human has an open-refrigerator policy for the hedonistic Scorpio dog, this could work. A Taurus is soothing and grounding for the emotionally strung-out Scorpio poochie. In turn, the Scorpio is passionately loyal to the Taurus. The Scorpio dog pulls the Taurus human out of all of his favorite and deeply entrenched ruts. Taurus human does not like this one bit. Doggie better simmer down before smoke comes out of Taurus human's nose.

A SCORPIO DOG WITH A GEMINI OWNER

All the yakety-yak might make the Scorpio dog think the Gemini's a little wack. The Scorpio dog is the strong, silent type, which makes the nervous Gemini want to fill the quiet space with chatter. The Scorpio needs private time, but with the Gemini human running the house, it's more likely to feel like Grand Central station. A Scorpio dog demands your undivided attention but with the Gemini's ADD, he's likely to forget the Scorpio's name or existence. If Gemini can get with the program, there is hope for this pair: They'll find a common bond in their love for extremes. These two should try skydiving together.

A SCORPIO DOG WITH A CANCER OWNER

There's an instinctive bond between these two: Both dog and owner are super-sensitive with emotions running high and low, so they'll be able to tolerate each other's internal stormy weather. This is one of those "it's you and me against the world" matches; the Cancer human will be ultra-protective of the Scorpio pup as though she were a human child. The Scorpio has no problem being mothered and smothered as long as she gets some alone time.

A SCORPIO DOG WITH A LEO OWNER

Both take pride in their strength and nobility of character. The only difference is that the Leo human flaunts it. A Scorpio dog prefers the subtle approach and may sometimes look askance at the Leo's constant fishing for compliments. Then again, the Scorpio is so adoring of her owner that the Leo won't have to fish too much. There may just be the occasional conflict of wills with this control freak combo. But there's still hope for the match: The Scorpio loves the Leo's lust for life and five-star restaurants. The Scorpio needs to be top dog; the loyal Leo wouldn't have it any other way. The Leo human would run, not walk, when the Scorpio calls, which is this dog's number-one requirement.

A SCORPIO DOG WITH A VIRGO OWNER

These two are like Felix and Oscar, but they love and appreciate the differences between each other. The Scorpio dog runs on nerves and feelings—the Virgo just runs on nerves. Both have impossibly high standards that mere mortals could never really meet. The Scorpio pup appreciates the Virgo's mental acuity and sharp analysis, just so long as she doesn't bust the cat out of the bag, ruining the Scorpio's little secrets.

A SCORPIO DOG WITH A LIBRA OWNER

Libra's polished ways will soothe the highest-strung Scorpio's nerves. But watch out when the Libra human enters wishy-washy mode: the Scorpio dog will wince, whine, and whimper in disgust. While the Libra's busy weighing all the options, the Scorpio will fume over the lack of attention. A Scorpio needs singular devotion; at first, a Libra might find this pup too demanding. Ever the peacemaker, the

✳

Libra will insist on making this dog-human balancing act work—and the Scorpio dog will reward him with an endless supply of devotion.

A Scorpio Dog with a Scorpio Owner

Perhaps the most potent pairing in the entire zodiac, when this dog-human combo is good, it's very good; but when it's bad—look out! This is the kind of love that runs much deeper than human-human love; nothing will ever come between these two, including death. One love, one heart; once these two die-hards get together, they'll feel all right.

A Scorpio Dog with a Sagittarius Owner

The serious Scorpio pooch could use some of a Sag human's goofiness. The Scorpio dog finds Sag's bluntness and clumsiness embarrassing at the dog run; the Sag is just clowning around but the Scorpio doesn't see the humor. The Sag human loves how a Scorpio pup thinks so deeply about things that wouldn't interest ordinary dogs. Both have a serious grass-is-greener complex; both want what others have and think more is always better. Their shared road of excess could involve some backlash.

A Scorpio Dog with a Capricorn Owner

The down-to-earth Capricorn human will let the Scorpio dog be her more brooding self. They'll be instantly at ease with each other. Both have a great need for respect and go about it in a quiet, unassuming way. Both are shy and needy at heart but disguise it with self-sufficiency. The Scorpio knows she's in good hands with this Rock of Gibraltar human. The pragmatic Cap knows he made the right choice with such a no-nonsense, sophisticated pooch.

A Scorpio Dog with an Aquarius Owner

Perhaps it's not such a wise idea for these two wild and rebellious creatures to get together—life will be a series of unexpected upheavals. Then again, both the Scorpio doggie and Aquarian human march to the beat of their own drummers: This could work as long as the neighbors don't mind the clashing symphonies. These two might seem like two ships passing in the night, but both pick up psychic signals from outer space, both need long periods of alone time, both are quirky and generally misunderstood . . . you get the idea. This is the odd couple incarnate. Keep the hair dryers away from the tub.

A Scorpio Dog with a Pisces Owner

This dog-human match is like a dream: the intense Scorpio dog will dig the Pisces human's la-la land. As long as this includes regular feedings and walks, the Scorpio pooch will feel like life with the Pisces is heaven on earth. If the Pisces completely loses touch with reality and forgets the Scorpio's daily rituals, this pup might have a hard time overlooking such neglect. The Pisces human will have no choice but to get her act together, or out of guilt she'll overcompensate by spoiling Scorpio with more bones than he can handle.

TYPICAL SCORPIO BREEDS

German Shepherd, Doberman Pinscher, and Rhodesian Ridgeback

STAR SIGHTING: ZUKI—GERMAN SHEPHERD

The most powerful and intense canine on Earth, the German shepherd is by far the most trusted cop dog in the world. This dog takes loyalty and courage to a whole other level; you can count on her to sacrifice her own life for you in a heartbeat. She's so intelligent that she could probably run your household with one paw, but she's also smart enough to leave the mundane human stuff for you. She has more important things to think about.

This serious thinker can also be a giant goofball, especially when she's surrounded by her favorite people. Since this dog was originally bred for herding, be sure to train and socialize her early on, for she can be overly protective of her family (her sheep) and quite wary of strangers. German shepherds can also be possessive and jealous; like the Scorpions, they love you enough to die for you and expect the same devotion in return. Think again before you bring another pet into the home.

REAL-LIFE EXAMPLES OF GERMAN SHEPHERDS/ SCORPIO TRAITS

- Zuki casually walks in front of the camera whenever her mommy tries to photograph the family cat.
- Zuki is so jealous of her new brother, Kato, their parents are forced to take them on separate walks.

✳

9

DOG STAR

Sagittarius

(November 22 – December 21)

THE SAGITTARIUS DOG

ELEMENT: Fire

MODALITY: Mutable

RULERSHIP: Jupiter

SYMBOL: Archer

MOST COMPATIBLE WITH: Libra, Aquarius, Aries, and Leo

WHAT A SAG DOG DAYDREAMS ABOUT: the emerald-green grass on the other end of the rainbow . . . with the biggest dog park and his own private jet

KEYWORDS: gregarious, fun-loving, optimistic, adventurous, free-spirited, goofy, and clumsy

THE SAGITTARIUS
DOG STAR'S PERSONALITY

⚲ The Sag dog needs open air and convertible rides.

⚲ The Sag dog needs constant excitement and greener pastures.

⚲ The Sag dog needs to bark it like it is.

⚲ The Sag dog needs positivity and joy.

⚲ The Sag dog needs the carnival and parades.

⚲ The Sag dog needs rainbows to chase and dreams to dream.

⚲ The Sag dog needs to travel long distances.

⚲ The Sag dog needs freedom.

⚲ The Sag dog loves to explore, know, and understand.

STAR SIGN CHARACTERISTICS

LUCKY CHARM

Like a comet with a furry tail, Sagittarius is the luckiest Dog Star in the zodiac. This cheerful Pollyanna of a pup will be the shining beacon of the household. Forget your gloom-and-doom mentality: A Sag prefers to look on the bright side of things and think positive thoughts. Yes, she is forever chasing bees and rainbows but that's what makes her joy so contagious. And besides, she actually finds the gold at the end—even after the Capricorn and Scorpio doggies look at her skeptically. The Sag

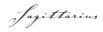

dog doesn't care; she knows that if she can dream about it, it's possible. She loves sprinting through the dog runs and parks and can't stand to be caged for even one second. This pup was born to be wild and born to run—even if she trips over her own two front paws once in a while (Sags are famously clumsy little creatures). Her boundless enthusiasm, a certain joie de vivre, is the envy of the other brooding dog stars. She loves all things foreign and expects you to take her on frequent overseas trips. She needs to expand her horizons. Sure, she suffers from the grass is greener complex, but that just means she needs longer walks to explore what's just over yonder. Then she can return home knowing that she really prefers her own backyard.

Dog Run

This dog never slows down. She's got an agenda and it's called Living with a capital L. Life is a holiday complete with fantastic adventures and doggie treats 365 days a year. The Sag needs plenty of room to roam. She'll prefer country living with expansive grounds to explore. If you're not careful, this roaming pooch might wander off and dig her way to China. Like the Gemini Dog Star, this dog goes stir crazy in an instant. Make sure you give her major breathing space. Don't box a Sag dog into a room the size of your shower or she will literally start to climb the walls or assault you by barking swear words through her teeth when you come home. If you're going to coop this dog up in a small space, it better be in a pet carrier to actually go somewhere! The Sag dog would really adore you if you'd let her ride in the main cabin with you. She wants to see out the window; she wants to see everything! The Sag pooch has big dreams, grand visions of vacations and more vacations. Speak to her in a foreign language and she'll melt.

✳

A WISE DOG KNOWS HE'S A FOOL

If Shakespeare wrote a play about dogs, the Sag would be the fool. She'd gladly dance around wagging a bell on her tail. Sag loves parties, amusement parks, carnivals, and the circus: anything that's fun and larger than life. Don't you know life is for smiling, laughing, and pleasure? A Sag will teach you how it's done. Forget your human worries and take a jog around the park, a nonstop flight to Europe and back, a trek across the Himalayas—why, this dog would love to be an astronaut's best friend. Or if you don't have a travel budget, why not throw a block party for her and all of her puppy friends? But don't forget to play world music and stuff the piñatas full of Greenies. Sag dogs have a real extravagant streak and do not believe in moderation—especially when it comes to food. Don't be surprised if she has an ever-expanding girth to match her boundless nature. A true free spirit in every sense, you'll notice that she doesn't take well to training or being told what to do. For a Sag doggie, it's her way or the highway. You'll have to go with the flow or she'll develop a canine hitchhiker's thumb. She can't stand the feeling of restraint. Freedom or bust!

IF THE SAGITTARIUS DOG COULD TALK

JetBlue is having a sale.

Um, I'd prefer a sportier collar.

I'll take the high road, thank you.

I meant to do that.

The squeaky wheel gets the grease—and the squeaky dog gets the treats!

The truth will set you free.

What speed limit?

I'm not tired yet.

Oh, lighten up!

Life is too short! Let's live it up!

WHAT A SAGITTARIUS DOG WANTS IN AN OWNER

FREE BIRD

I need a fellow free spirit, a lover of the open road. My very own Jack Kerouac. If you've racked up a zillion frequent flyer miles, I'll adore you. You can take me with you on all of your overseas trips. We'll stay in the finest exotic hotels and see all the sights. I'll be the dog companion of your roaming gypsy soul. I need a human with a large open space, preferably in a woodsy area where I can sniff around without getting bored. I can't stand being locked up in small spaces with no windows. I need outdoor access! I want to lie in the grass with you and stare at the big blue sky. Do you love nature as much as I do? Will you take me camping with you? If you have an RV or a convertible, I think we are destined for each other.

✳

DEEP THOUGHTS WITH JACK DOGGY

Are you a philosopher or a deeply spiritual human? I totally dig that. Do you like to rock out? I'm down with that. I'm a little bit country and a little bit rock 'n' roll. Are you a little bit of a gypsy or a hippie? For us, life will be like one grand Celebrity cruise. Then again, if you're all work and no play, you'll make me one pathetic pooch. Vacation is my middle name—I live for the festivities. Don't you dare dampen my spirits with your pessimistic notions: Who says life has to be hard? (Some Capricorn Dog Star, probably.) I say life is meant to be savored like the finest wine. Some may accuse me of being a Pollyanna pooch, always seeing the bright side and chasing rainbows when I'm not chasing my own tail. The more optimistic you are, the more I wag.

POLICY OF TRUTH

I need an owner who will come home when she says she will. Truth is the most important virtue a human being could possibly have in my book, so if I catch you feeding me even little white lies, I'll give you the sad puppy eyes to let you know I'm disappointed that you did not tell the truth. The more honest and forthright you live your life, the more I bark for joy! I can spot a liar and a thief from miles away so if you don't want me growling, don't bring any shyster characters around our honest home, *s'il vous plait*.

HOW TO EARN BROWNIES POINTS
FROM A SAGITTARIUS DOGGIE

Fast cars	20 pts
Frequent outings	20 pts
Long-distance trips	20 pts
Lots of birdie toys	20 pts
Soccer ball, tennis balls, volleyball, baseball, etc.	20 pts
	100 pts

COMPATIBILITY GUIDE

Most Compatible with: Libra, Aquarius, Aries, and Leo

A SAGITTARIUS DOG WITH AN ARIES OWNER

Awesome and exhilarating, this match is a wild and crazy joy ride as long as both learn to curb their accident-prone tendencies. The Aries human will love a Sag dog's big outlook on life. Why do anything if it doesn't cause a racket? Both dog and human live a little dangerously, like two kamikaze pioneers, which is exciting: but hide the matches or they'll burn down the house. This is the bona fide party combo of the pack.

✳

A SAGITTARIUS DOG WITH A TAURUS OWNER

This bon vivant pooch needs an equally bubbly owner—so where does the no-nonsense, practical Taurus owner come in? Hopefully nowhere. Unless the Taurus human plans to loosen up and go a little spastic now and then, this speedy pup will likely wear him out within forty-eight hours max. A Sag dog can't stand being grounded and a Taurus human would rather *not* be flying. But there is hope for this pair: If the Taurus can muster some courage to explore, the Sag dog will teach him that there's much more to life than eating and sleeping.

A SAGITTARIUS DOG WITH A CANCER OWNER

A true Sag doggie will want to leave the nest rather than be smothered by the Cancer human's domesticating and overly protective ways. A Cancer will want to jump off a bridge if she has to endure the antics of this happy-dappy dog for too long. Why all of the prancing around with glee for no reason? The Cancer's brooding will dampen doggie's spirits. A Cancer likes to build a dark, cozy den; the Sag considers this Hades on earth. But in the end, the Sag doggie could be just what the Cancer needs to get out of the house and actually see the world in the sunshine for once.

A SAGITTARIUS DOG WITH A LEO OWNER

An exciting little duet of jet-setting pleasure seekers! Extravagance: That's their motto. This fiery couple doesn't do anything halfway. Life is a pleasure and the Leo human knows how to ride in a flashy convertible with the top down. The vivacious Sag dog complements the Leo's flair for the dramatic. The Sag will inspire the Leo to make movies in foreign languages in exotic places, or at the very least

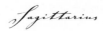

to get bigger and bolder. There's always another horizon to explore, another chart to top. This match deserves a standing ovation.

A Sagittarius Dog with a Virgo Owner

Worrywart Virgo human will have a Sag dog chasing her tail, and not in a good way. The Sag doggie doesn't want to sweat the details; does it matter if the house is messy when there's so much to see and do outside? It's difficult for a Sag to tolerate such pickiness in a human. The Virgo human also wants to keep his pooch on a short leash and the Sag pup needs to run free. The Virgo appreciates the Sag doggie's expansive mind and spiritual leanings, but the Sag doggie's boundless energy might tie the nervous Virgo up in knots. When the Virgo's ready to throw in the towel, the Sag will remind him that sometimes laughter is the best medicine. And there is no shortage of that with a goofy Sag dog.

A Sagittarius Dog with a Libra Owner

A Libra human will keep her Sagittarius doggie out of trouble in balanced ways; the Sag reminds the Libra that sometimes important decisions can be put off till tomorrow: Life is too short, there's too much fun to be had! Both love socializing, both love nature, and good food. The Libra would never feed the Sag doggie generic food. She believes that everyone, whether dog or human, deserves only the finest. It's got to be opulent with this duo.

A Sagittarius Dog with a Scorpio Owner

The Sag pup is here to save the day! The Scorpio human forgets how to just have fun. What's the point of holding on to the past when there's so much new green grass to explore and roll around in? The Scorpio will worship this little spiritual seeker; the Sag will open up this introverted human's eyes to new experiences. This pair is a nice blend of extremes as long as the Sag doesn't bark too much. The Scorpio human will put up with a Sag dog's thirst for adventure as long as they can keep a low profile

A Sagittarius Dog with a Sagittarius Owner

Two clowns, two explorers, two truth seekers: This is a match for big dreams and endless journeys. The Sag human understands this dog's every need without even a bark between them. Together life is exactly how they like it: one big party with a rolling expanse of fortune and gluttony. But since neither will know when to say when and when to curb their enthusiasm, there will be credit card debts to pay and pounds to shed. Then again, with their luck, they'll win the lotto and bounce right back.

A Sagittarius Dog with a Capricorn Owner

The Capricorn is much too serious for a fun-loving Sag doggie. It's sunny outside, throw me a squeaky toy, put the work down for a second, and run around with me! On the other hand, the Sag dog will appreciate the Capricorn's hard work when it comes to buying expensive doggie treats and things to play with. Still, the Cap human needs to lighten up enough to actually enjoy her smiling, effusive dog and step out of work mode long enough to sniff the roses.

A Sagittarius Dog with an Aquarius Owner

These two are like a fun-filled home entertainment package. The Sag doggie loves how the Aquarius breaks convention; the Aquarius appreciates the Sag's enthusiasm and eternal optimism. Life is one big sprawling, expansive journey with lots of interesting people and experiences to savor. A Sag doggie might expect her human to run around a little more than the Aquarius would like, but at least the exercise will keep them both in good shape.

A Sagittarius Dog with a Pisces Owner

Both have big dreams, both have wishes and hopes and want the world to be a better place. The only problem is that the Sag doggie actually wants the dreams to become a reality; the Pisces doesn't really see the difference between dream and reality. If the Pisces human is into nature and spiritual pilgrimage, then this Sag doggie seeker will be happy to walk beside her. Both have visions of something far beyond the scope of human and dog experience. The Pisces human will have to set her alarm for the Sag doggie's daily long jogs unless she lives in a farm where her free-spirited friend can run and chase till sundown.

TYPICAL SAGITTARIUS BREEDS

German Shorthaired pointer, Boxer, and Brittany Spaniel

STARS SIGHTING: ZOE AND CORA— GERMAN SHORTHAIRED POINTERS

Not only do they point like an archer, German Shorthaired pointers also burst with energy like the typical Sagittarians. Exuberant, quick, powerful, happy-go-lucky, tolerant, enthusiastic, smart, alert, affectionate, gentle, even-tempered, and

✳

responsive: This dog is a perfect date if you are a fun-loving human. Couch potatoes need not even consider this restless character.

GSPs were originally bred for hunting but have also become popular as family companions because of their sweet nature. Versatile and adaptable, they'll fit in with any lifestyle, as long as you keep them active. GSPs need *exercise!* They love to run, chase, and run—and chase and run some more. A tired GSP is a happy GSP.

You'll rarely find an unfriendly GSP; like Sags, they're usually made of sugar and will love everyone they meet. However, they can become extremely excitable and could knock small children over.

REAL-LIFE EXAMPLES OF GERMAN SHORTHAIRED POINTERS/SAGITTARIUS TRAITS

- Cora (opposite) divides her unconditional love by giving everyone in her family an equal amount of lap time whether they're at the dining table or watching TV in the family room.
- Zoe (page 122) does the same even when she's visiting neighbors and friends.
- Both ladies can outrun cheetahs.

10

DOG STAR

Capricorn

(December 22 – January 19)

THE CAPRICORN DOG

ELEMENT: Earth

MODALITY: Cardinal

RULERSHIP: Saturn

SYMBOL: Goat

MOST COMPATIBLE WITH: Taurus, Virgo, Scorpio, and Pisces

WHAT A CAPRICORN DOG DAYDREAMS ABOUT: A high position in life—preferably the penthouse; being the CEO of the dog run

KEYWORDS: ambition, high standards, status, discipline, tradition, structure, rules, limits, authority, duty, responsibility, practical

THE CAPRICORN DOG STAR'S PERSONALITY

♑ The Capricorn dog needs to feel very accomplished.

♑ The Capricorn dog needs to feel in control.

♑ The Capricorn dog needs a sense of status.

♑ The Capricorn dog needs a fat bank account.

♑ The Capricorn dog needs security and simplicity.

♑ The Capricorn dog needs to feel like the head honcho.

♑ The Capricorn dog needs respect.

STAR SIGN CHARACTERISTICS

DOGGIE WARBUCKS

The Louis Vuitton of Dog Stars, Capricorn wants nothing more than status and success. This dog screams gold; she'd outdo any contestant on *The Apprentice* with her business acumen. She prefers to live in high-rises in big cities like big corporate execs. A Capricorn is a high-end dog. Her motto is, "Always go first cabin." She works hard to earn her prestige—so you'd better treat her right. Superbly disciplined, this focused poochie could teach slacker humans a thing or two about getting their ducks in order. She is the canine master of time and space. Time is money and she will teach you how to spend both wisely. She has big dreams and lofty ambitions. She wants to earn your respect through hard work and dedication. The Capricorn dog doesn't laugh too often, she smirks: Her signature stoic look is just a sign of dignity and purpose. Don't mistake it for depression or a mood disorder and waste time trying to cheer her up by buying her expensive treats and doggie toys. Look closely and you'll see the twinkle in her eye. Life is a game; she just appears to take it all seriously. Inside she is laughing all the way to the doggie bank.

CRACK THAT WHIP

If you haven't figured it out yet, the Capricorn Dog Star has extremely high standards. Of course, more clueless humans will fail to meet them. If she appears to be judging you ruthlessly in her little furry head, she probably is. Get used to it. The cosmos has sent you your very own taskmaster; this ethical pooch would never let you out of work to go golfing. You'd better get it together with this dog monitoring your every move. A Capricorn is bred from the highest moral order and will expect the same of you. She won't appreciate any skimping on her well-deserved long walks in her Gucci carrier. She works hard for you and expects to be reimbursed accordingly. Soon she'll be asking for a promotion from yucky dog bed to sofa to your bed because of her spotless record. She thrives on positive reinforcement, so be sure to give her serious acknowledgment for her good behavior. The surefire way to a Capricorn doggie's heart is with a good upgrade.

MORALITY BITES

A Capricorn Dog Star rarely messes in the house, chews furniture, or barks for no reason. She is self-possessed, self-contained, elegant, and poised. The Capricorn seems to get younger as she gets older because she has a guilt-free conscience. Everything is out in the open and aboveboard with this pragmatic pooch. She won't even sneak food when you're not looking. She'll wait for your approval instead. She lives by the

✳

highest moral order and will very often be the role model for less evolved doggies to follow. Other dog owners will marvel at how precocious and wise your Capricorn Dog Star is. Without uttering a bark, this sage of a dog speaks volumes with the timeless knowledge in her eyes. You'll never have to worry about inculcating this dog into the ways of civilized behavior because dignity and reserve are like second nature.

OBEY YOUR MASTER

This dog is the most patient and mature of all the Dog Stars—so thank your lucky stars that you got yourself such an effortless gem of a canine. This dog can practically take care of herself. This Dog Star is so adult, you may sometimes wonder if your Capricorn child is parenting you and not the other way around. She provides her owner with a reassuring, steady, and solid-as-a-rock sensibility. Just being around this dog suddenly makes you want to pay your bills on time and start your own Fortune 500 business. Certainly this Dog Star has come to inspire you to achieve much greater prominence in your career than you ever thought possible. That's because she is sending you subtle subliminal coaching 24/7—like your very own Anthony Robbins on four legs.

IF THE CAPRICORN DOG COULD TALK

Time is precious. I can't believe you're making me wait for this walk.

We need a plan here.

I'm not into shabby chic.

You should be ashamed of yourself.

I wouldn't touch that brand of dog food with a ten-foot pole.

This carrier is not functional.

Get with the program.

Have you no morals?

My daddy is the CEO of a very important company.

I worked very hard to get to where I am today.

WHAT A CAPRICORN DOG WANTS IN AN OWNER

GQ

I need a gentleman's gentleman. My ideal is a real sophisticated metrosexual. I prefer male to female owners, but if you're a lady I expect you to be well groomed, poised, and the CEO of your company. Slackers truly get under my fur. I need someone who appreciates living a very devout and disciplined existence. *There is no time like the present* and *the devil will find work for idle hands* are my two favorite mottoes. I can't abide someone who tries to live without any moral code. Anarchy is my worst fear. I revere tradition in conduct and furnishings.

✳

STATUS SYMBOL

I need someone who believes in hard work and as a result is successful—you know—well to do so you can afford to give me the finest dog bed, designer carriers, and gourmet dog food. I need to live a civilized existence, preferably in a penthouse or large estate. I scoff at poor manners and other such tacky displays by more ignorant doggies or humans. If you must know, I secretly love shopping with you in the finest department stores. Please don't forget to spray some of that designer fragrance on me. Beautiful workmanship makes me feel that the world is a safe place. It's all about the quality with me. I don't care how many cheap imitations you own: I want the real thing. I need someone with the highest standards: My worst fear is mediocrity. Poverty and homelessness are a close second. My doggie soul is used to a dignified life—I have been around the block enough times to know.

If you run a tight ship, you're my kind of parent. I appreciate the kind of human who has a totally reliable rhythm. I want to be able to set my doggie watch by you. You never keep me hanging or questioning whether you will come through for me. Of course, I'm too self-contained to play the victim so should you forget to feed me, I'll patiently wait for you to figure out your big debauch. I'm not one to name names but I do take notice. Deep down I believe I could do a better job than most adult humans—if only I was given the opportunity, I'd knock your socks off. I'll respect you forever if you stick to your routine and act like the most upstanding parent possible.

HOW TO EARN BROWNIE POINTS
FROM A CAPRICORN DOGGIE

Luxe apartment	20 pts
High-end doggie apparel	20 pts
Gourmet food	20 pts
Fat piggy bank	20 pts
First-class grooming	20 pts
	100 pts

COMPATIBILITY GUIDE

Most compatible with: Taurus, Virgo, Scorpio, and Pisces

A CAPRICORN DOG WITH AN ARIES OWNER

"Sweet Jesus, who is this uncouth human!!?" shrieks the Capricorn dog. *"Why does this puppy act like an old fogey?!"* exclaims the Aries human. Not wise to put these two in a room together for more than ten minutes, since fur will fly. This is like the old practical sage meets Winnie the Pooh or a bad pay-per-view showdown you don't really want to watch. The Capricorn will pretend she's never even met this loud-mouthed human. The Aries could lose his temper and treat the poor Capricorn doggie like a punching bag.

✳

A Capricorn Dog with a Taurus Owner

This sensible pair has oodles in common and they'll feel their kinship right off the bat. They share a love for piggy banks, fine cuisine, and Monopoly, of course. The Capricorn doggie may suffer from considerable weight gain by mooching off the Taurus human's five-meal-a-day plan and from cleaning up after the Taurus human's potato chip droppings around the La-Z-Boy. But as long as they end up filthy rich, each can let the little things slide.

A Capricorn Dog with a Gemini Owner

Even as a puppy, the Capricorn doggie tends to play the grown-up in this relationship. The Gemini human doesn't understand why the Capricorn doesn't just magically feed and walk himself when the Gemini is caught in the midst of a huge gabfest on the cell phone. The Capricorn Dog Star is appalled by how the Gemini human can turn into a total space cadet and walk out of the store without her. But the loyal Capricorn loves a challenge and being a Gemini's dog is like trying to scale Everest—the perfect goal for any hard-working Capricorn doggie.

A Capricorn Dog with a Cancer Owner

Both are a couple of lovable grumps with soft hearts beneath their tough exteriors. The Capricorn doggie can't bear to watch the bleeding-heart Cancer cry over sappy commercials. The Cancer human doesn't understand why the Capricorn dog feels guilty sleeping on her beautiful dog bed and prefers to tough it out on the cold linoleum floor. The Capricorn wishes she could get a job to support her Cancer human so he could just stay home and cook and play house.

A Capricorn Dog with a Leo Owner

The Leo human brings home the luxe doggie apparel, appealing to Capricorn's materialistic side. The Capricorn doggie is über-sophisticated and refined, which boosts the Leo's image for his grand entrances both on and off the red carpet. The Leo human is strong and hard working—two qualities a Capricorn pooch admires most. The Capricorn looks expensive—which allows the Leo to keep up the "rich and famous" persona he so adores.

A Capricorn Dog with a Virgo Owner

These two like to clean and organize together. Even daily walks are a whole dog and pony show, requiring hours of planning and prep before they even get out the door. The Virgo owner is sometimes guilty of overshampooing her Capricorn doggie and the Capricorn can't stand wasting shampoo or time or anything for that matter. The Virgo will just throw in the towel and expect serious Capricorn to clean up after himself, but of course the Virgo will give in because she doesn't want little paw prints all over the white carpet.

A Capricorn Dog with a Libra Owner

These two will have a hard time finding something in common, except that they grate on each other's nerves. The Libra human avoids the Capricorn because he detests nothing more than being judged. The Capricorn doggie despises how codependent the Libra is with his latest crush, neglecting the Capricorn's grooming schedule. Why can't the grouchy Capricorn just stop growling and make the Libra look pretty? If this pair could stop judging and avoiding for a minute,

*

they might discover that their love for fine art, food—well, for the finest of everything—will ease their troubles away.

A Capricorn Dog with a Scorpio Owner

Both revel in their own sarcasm and growl at other dogs and humans for no good reason. Both love to play the strong, silent type when they find you stupid or boring. Both love to have power over everyone. The Scorpio human loves that the Capricorn doggie is her right-hand dog, talking the Scorpio off the ledge time after time. The Capricorn is intrigued with the Scorpio human's choice of dog toys, like a voodoo doll of a cheating ex-lover. This is a solid match—as long as they keep the sarcastic fun under control and don't plow over the other doggies and humans around them.

A Capricorn Dog with a Sagittarius Owner

The Capricorn dog can't believe his grave misfortune of having been chosen by Bozo the Clown. The Sag human doesn't understand why this dog insists on smoking cigars and discussing finances. The Sag is at a loss for what to do with a dog that refuses to laugh, lick, shake hands, or do back flips. The Capricorn dog has more important things to do than coddle this overzealous happy freak. At first, the Sag human will want to export this killjoy canine to Timbuktu or put him on Prozac—but then he'll look at the bright side (as always) and realize that it's his mission to teach the Capricorn a few things about enjoying life. And this hard-working doggie will appreciate the Sag's sincere efforts.

Capricorn

A CAPRICORN DOG WITH A CAPRICORN OWNER

Finally, a dog that actually enjoys listening to Capricorn's earnest discussion of his 401(K) for hours on end. Both share the same kind of no-nonsense, nuts-and-bolts, bare-bones, nitty-gritty philosophy of life—the kind that keeps hair/fur on your chest and coins in your bank account. The Capricorn human loves that this pooch is inherently disciplined. The Capricorn dog loves that he doesn't have to waste any precious time on training this human. It's nothing but up, up, up for this pair.

A CAPRICORN DOG WITH AN AQUARIUS OWNER

The Capricorn dog does not take kindly to having her fur dyed pink. The Aquarius owner gets fed up with the Capricorn's scoffing at gluten-free dog food. A Capricorn dog needs rules, structure, and order in the home. An Aquarius is like *"Say what?"* Who needs rules when they're meant to be broken? The Aquarius human likes to dress the Capricorn doggie in activist T-shirts and parade her around in front of the White House. The Cap doggie is fine with such shenanigans as long as there's something productive to do. The Aquarius owner has no recourse but to dye the Capricorn's fur in multicolors for kicks.

A CAPRICORN DOG WITH A PISCES OWNER

The Capricorn dog quickly gets tired of playing alarm clock for the Pisces human, who habitually oversleeps. The Pisces grows weary of the Cap's constant brooding over the credit card debt. Wait, the Pisces can't find her Cap doggie again: Is she buried under the pile of dirty clothes or under the stack of dishes that the Pisces

✳

forgot to take out of the bed? This upstanding doggie is the angel of structure and discipline, which the Pisces human so desperately needs.

TYPICAL CAPRICORN BREEDS

Yorkshire Terrier, Bernese Mountain Dog, and Schnauzer

STAR SIGHTING: KIKI—YORKSHIRE TERRIER

No other theme song says it better: This social-climbing, "I've earned my way up," pragmatic little diva is the most hard-working and disciplined Dog Star of the zodiac. Whether it is the highest mountain or the most prestigious doggie status, the Goat will most likely make their way to the top. Yorkies were originally bred by working men in northern England to catch rodents. They were miniaturized over the years and climbed their way up to become the high-society fashion statement they are today.

Loyal, loving, spirited, alert, and playful, this little pooch can also be quite demanding and stubborn. They need structure and routine early on and it may take some effort on the owner's part to housebreak them. Like most Capricorns, they are shy with new people and need to spend some time warming up to them. Yorkies, due to their little size, are much better with older and considerate children than with small children who could hurt them easily. They are wonderful apartment dogs but require nothing less than first-class grooming.

REAL-LIFE EXAMPLES OF YORKSHIRE TERRIER/ CAPRICORN TRAITS

- Kiki lives in a penthouse apartment in San Francisco with a view worth a million bucks.
- Kiki prefers to stay inside her deluxe apartment but on occasional outings, she gets carried around in her fancy carrier and refuses to walk on the ground.
- Unlike most other dogs who will beg for any attention, strangers need to earn Kiki's affection. Once you pass her warm-up test, she will give you nothing but love and respect.

11

DOG STAR

Aquarius

(January 20 – February 18)

THE AQUARIUS DOG

ELEMENT: Air

MODALITY: Fixed

RULERSHIP: Uranus

SYMBOL: Water Bearer

MOST COMPATIBLE WITH: Gemini, Libra, Aries, and Sagittarius

WHAT AN AQUARIAN DOG DAYDREAMS ABOUT: a house full of the most wonderful freaks and geeks imaginable; a dog run full of friendsters

KEYWORDS: eccentric, independent, free-thinker, radical, friendly, people-lover, unpredictable, aloof, erratic, nervous, high-strung

THE AQUARIUS DOG STAR'S PERSONALITY

≈ The Aquarius dog needs to shake up the status quo.

≈ The Aquarius dog wants a wild troupe of doggie and people friends.

≈ The Aquarius dog needs dreams and goals to chase.

≈ The Aquarius dog likes to experiment and come up with new crazy inventions.

≈ The Aquarius dog likes to shock your socks off.

≈ The Aquarius dog wants freedom at all costs.

≈ The Aquarius dog loves surprises.

STAR SIGN CHARACTERISTICS

THE ORIGINAL MAN'S BEST FRIEND

Everyone wants the Aquarius dog to be his or her best friend. So effortlessly cool and easy to get along with, this dog will love you regardless of your age, race, background, or class. The weirder the better, as far as an Aquarius Dog Star is concerned. Equal parts genius and equal parts doggie, this is the quirkiest and most easily lovable companion on the block. Though this pooch might seem aloof at first meeting, soon you'll see she has the most genuine spirit you could want in a best friend. She's always up for adventures, is knowledgeable about most things

technical, and cares deeply about humanitarian issues. If you need help downloading ring tones, want to talk about international politics, or need a companion
for the next big rally, an Aquarius is the dog for you. Like a Libra, the Aquarius
wants everyone to get along. The more the merrier is easily her motto. She'll be
loyally devoted but don't expect the Aquarius to smother you with affection like
the dutiful Leo might. She's content just sitting by your side, practicing mental
telepathy or trying to figure out the next big innovation. It's no wonder so many
Aquarians are in the hall of fame. They receive streaks of genius from out of
nowhere. If you see your pooch off in space, don't try to rein her back in because
she is most likely just figuring out the next discovery in quantum physics. This
doggie will forever keep you on your toes. You'll never quite know what to expect
but your life will be one happy, bizarre string of random surprises, which keeps
things interesting.

Barking to the Beat of My Own Drummer

This dog stands out from the crowd with her unique signature style. The best way
to spot an Aquarius dog star is by her quirky, off-beat style, whether it's an outlandish dog collar or her eccentric doggie mannerisms. Your Aquarian Dog Star
might even twitch or have sudden bursts of energy where she shoots around the
house like a bolt of lightning. Expect the unexpected with this outlandish pooch.
They live by their own weirdo rules that change for no apparent rhyme or reason.
Don't try to figure this doggie out, because its utterly impossible. This dog defies the
laws of normal human gravity and logic—you'd have to be a rocket scientist yourself to truly decode the brilliant behaviors of this mad scientist dog. You see,

✳

Aquarian doggies are simply light-years ahead of the rest of us mere mortals, so the best you can hope for is that some of her oddball genius will rub off on you when you bathe and brush her. Watch and learn, you'll uncover the secrets to the universe.

I-POOCH

An Aquarius Dog Star is a four-legged megabyte of information. They're astonishingly bright: if only they came with a printer. Like little Greek philosophers and modern inventors rolled into one, they're tech geniuses; heck, they could probably fix your computer if you'd let them. When they appear to be napping they're actually downloading every nano-bit of information floating through the ether at that moment in time. It's as if these pups have internal wires connecting them directly to the information super highway. Their thoughts are light-years ahead of other less-evolved doggies and humans. All pups are unique, but the Aquarius seems like an entirely different species sent from an as-yet-undiscovered planet. They're like a blinking neon sign in a world full of run-of-the-mill painted storefronts, like a solar-powered mini on a road full of gas-guzzling SUVs, the polka-dotted pooch in a park full of solid-colored pups. They march to the beat of their own doggie drummer and will want to wear the most bizarre doggie costumes while they're doing it. Born rebels, they aren't fully happy unless they're stirring up the status quo. Nothing's more fun than shocking the socks off of you.

DON'T CRAMP MY STYLE, BUDDY

Sometimes the Aquarius dog's independence makes it seem like she needs nothing from you, but don't let that fool you. She needs people, minus the ones who would smother her to death. This dog prefers a nice casual group of punk rockers, hippies, social activists, and "girl and guy next door" types to pal around with. She isn't one of those possessive one-on-one types. She's happy knowing her best bud is nearby, but she'd prefer not to smell your human breath. Let her drift off into her own astral plane and glean the latest insights that will take the rest of humanity decades longer to understand. This people-person dog loves groups— the more people, the better! She'd join doggie science clubs and humane societies and political parties if she could. Aquarius dogs like to herd everyone together. They're highly civilized but unconventional: a big furball of contradictions. One minute they'll seem like the most average Joe dog and the next, like a genius freak from Mars. In any case, good luck finding a more conscious and conscientious canine. They're really here to save humanity from its own stupidity. Let this wise old dog teach you some new tricks.

IF THE AQUARIUS DOG COULD TALK

$E = mc^2$ dude.

No blood for oil! Save the baby seals!

I want a tattoo of Mickey Mouse on my forehead!

The purple man told me that the end is near, but near is far and far is wide and wide is . . . cantaloupe juice.

Let's have a party!

Why be normal?

When can I get some piercings?

I want that tie-dyed collar in the window!

Let's go to the protest!

I wag to the beat of my own drummer.

WHAT AN AQUARIUS DOG WANTS IN AN OWNER
BLIND ME WITH SCIENCE

You model your personality after my hero, Bill Maher. In other words, you're not afraid to go against the establishment and really speak your mind—*and* with a brilliant sense of humor. You're a leader, not a follower: a real individual, true to yourself with quirks and all. You don't give a fig what other people think about you. You do your own thing because that is who you are. You're not afraid of getting into trouble: you challenge authority. You'll let me pee in forbidden places or walk on the neighbor's lawn, just to test the limits of convention. You know that rules were meant to be broken. You're experimental: you even like to dye my hair pink or let me have a mohawk. I'm a tech freak so you'd better love gadgets, electronics, buy me a plasma TV, and take photos of me on the latest digital camera. I love watching television with you, but if you opt for the lowbrow nonsense news channels, we need to have a discussion! If you watch *Real Time* with my hero, we're set. I don't like mindless sitcoms either; I want to watch intelligent documentaries on *Animal Planet* or The Discovery Channel.

CROWD PLEASER

If you're the kind of down-to-earth and sensibly logical human being with decent morals, we'll get on great. I'm looking for a real buddy, a pal, a person who truly knows the definition of friendship. If you have a lot of interesting and strange friends yourself—all the better. I thrive in a crowd, and hope that you would consider my friends your friends, and your friends my friends. In other words, it's important that your friends have lots of pooches for me to play with. I prefer not to be an only pooch if you can help it. But if so, please be sure to take me to plenty of doggie social outings, ice cream socials, and dog-run mixers. I need to make friends and influence people. My tail starts to droop when I'm deprived of social stim for too long. Please, I beg of you, don't isolate me. I need people and more people and doggies and more doggies. Oh and as a little aside, I dig it when you dress me up in loud and eccentric doggie clothing. The wilder and more rebellious the better. I love loud prints and funky dog collars that make people go "hmmm." Whatever you do, please don't dress me like the other dogs on the block. I must, repeat—*must*—be my own dog.

HOW TO EARN BROWNIE POINTS
FROM AN AQUARIUS DOGGIE

New and innovative toys	20 pts
Daily social gatherings	20 pts
Weekly parties	20 pts

Rallies and protests	20 pts
Constant mental stimulation	20 pts
	100 pts

COMPATIBILITY GUIDE

Most compatible with: Gemini, Libra, Aries, Sagittarius

AN AQUARIUS DOG WITH AN ARIES OWNER

An Aries and an Aquarius make the rules up as they go. No one is going to tell these two headstrong characters what to do or how to do it. Sometimes the Aries human tries to boss around his Aquarian dog: but this lasts all of about .02 seconds. It's over as soon as the Aquarius turns around and gives the Aries the deep-freeze shoulder. There's nothing an Aries human hates more than being ignored, so the Aquarius doggie usually gets her way but the Aries human loves the challenge anyway.

AN AQUARIUS DOG WITH A TAURUS OWNER

The Aquarius dog needs Taurus to put down the French fries and go out for a walk; for crying out loud, why does it take so long to put the leash on and get some fresh air? And why does the Taurus human walk so slowly? And why does she always take the same path? The Taurus human needs the Aquarian Dog Star to stop it with the nervous twitch. But quirks aside, these two are bonded like glue. Besides, the Taurus human could use a dog so connected to the ethereal, whose

✳

brain zips around and brings the information down to earth (since the Taurus never leaves it).

AN AQUARIUS DOG WITH A GEMINI OWNER

The Aquarius dog is instantly enamored with this quick-witted Gemini human. Both have lightning-speed minds and can dance circles around the other signs. They'll love to jet around the town together, checking out all the geeks and freaks. They have a major telepathic connection: The Aquarius doesn't even mind when the Gemini puts words into his mouth. If he could speak he'd say the same things anyway.

AN AQUARIUS DOG WITH A CANCER OWNER

This doting human will mother and smother her Aquarius doggie a little too much for comfort. The Cancer human feels crushed by the Aquarian doggie's cold and detached ways. Both feel the other is from some other planet that they'd rather not visit. The Aquarius dog wants more freedom; the Cancer wants the Aquarius to need her, but this activist of a doggie is too busy saving the world. Cancer will have to be coddled elsewhere.

AN AQUARIUS DOG WITH A LEO OWNER

Aquarius doggies have enough personality to keep up with the hotshot Leo human. Both are eccentric in their own ways. The Aquarian dog plays it cool while the Leo gets crazy dramatic. Both love parties and clothes, though the Leo will have to loosen up a little and let the Aquarius sneak by the fashion police. The Aquarius dog teaches the Leo not to give a flying fig about what other people think; the Leo in turn shows the Aquarius that drama can sometimes be cool.

An Aquarius Dog with a Virgo Owner

This dog-human combo makes each other nervous. The Virgo spends too much time cleaning; the Aquarius just wants to mess it up for kicks. The Aquarius dog doesn't understand why everything has to be kept in its perfect little box with color-coded label. The Virgo will flip when the Aquarius starts marching around the park with every neighborhood dog barking behind them. If this is going to work, the Aquarius dog will have to make some human friends who can take him out for walks when the Virgo needs a little peace and quiet.

An Aquarius Dog with a Libra Owner

It can drive the Libra human a little crazy when the Aquarius dog tries to re-arrange his wardrobe so that he has to go to work with mismatched socks and a shirt and tie that clash. This dog is a bit unconventional for a Libra human's graceful ways. The rebel Aquarius will want to tilt the picture frames and scramble his playlist. However, they both love people and ultimately want the same things: like peace and harmony and all things idealistic. If the Libra can handle being thrown off balance and the Aquarius can curb some of his more outlandish ideas, then the world will smile on this match.

An Aquarius Dog with a Scorpio Owner

An Aquarius dog likes having such a deep human around. Together they'll study the great mysteries like UFOs and presidential conspiracy theories. The Scorpio human will definitely impress the Aquarius with her unique book collection and eccentric hobbies. The aloof Aquarius dog will give Scorpio enough space, but watch out when he brings home the whole dog park and their owners, too. The

Aquarius doesn't understand why the Scorpio doesn't love everyone as much as he does. How can a pooch be so possessive?

AN AQUARIUS DOG WITH A SAGITTARIUS OWNER

This combo sizzles like a hair dryer that fell into the bathtub—and liked it. The Sag lives life by the seat of his pants; the Aquarius will insist on the coolest threads so this dog can pick up all of the artists, humanitarians, activists, world travelers, et cetera, et cetera . . . it's a party bigger than every NGO in every nation when these two get together. While the Sag human is busy playing sports or waxing philosophical, the Aquarius will be booking the flight plans for their next big adventure or humanitarian project. Both get to have their freedom, both get to volley ideas back and forth, and they never, ever get bored.

AN AQUARIUS DOG WITH A CAPRICORN OWNER

The Capricorn human appreciates this doggie's idealism and superior intellect—but that's about it. The Aquarius dog is off at the sight of stodgy Capricorn's regimented food plan, walking schedule, and snobby social circle. Why do all of her friends have to be making six figures and using such cumbersome language? The Aquarius will try to foil the Capricorn's plans just to watch her face turn different shades of red; The Capricorn in turn will force the Aquarius to stay home from doggie gatherings with no TV for a month. With such different styles, this match might seem to spell disaster—but the Capricorn appreciates the Aquarius dog's lofty humanitarian goals and in the end the Aquarius is grateful for Cap's big bank account to fund them.

AN AQUARIUS DOG WITH AN AQUARIUS OWNER

This pair could win a political campaign single-handedly. The Aquarius dog will reign in the herd; the Aquarius human will spout lengthy debates from the dirt that the doggie kicked up. When they're not out barking/screaming their heads off at rallies or feeding the homeless, these two love to watch intellectual TV shows together and host costume theme parties for all of their quirky/artsy/nerdy friends.

AN AQUARIUS DOG WITH A PISCES OWNER

More than a little crazy, this is a match made in chaos—squared. The Pisces forgets to feed the Aquarius half the time, but this doggie's smart enough to figure out how to do it herself. The Aquarius doesn't mind if the Pisces gets lost in reveries; the Pisces knows that one day the Aquarius doggie will create the world she can only download in her furry head today.

TYPICAL AQUARIUS BREEDS

Cocker Spaniel, Beagle, and Siberian Husky

STAR SIGHTING: ANISSE, LOLA, AND SHIRAZ— COCKER SPANIELS

It's no coincidence that our favorite humanitarian, the ultimate Aquarian, Oprah, has chosen cocker spaniels as her most trusted cohorts. This playful, cheery, sweet,

loyal, gentle, charismatic, and trustworthy pooch is one of the most popular American breeds. Although they were originally bred for hunting wild game, these ladies are mostly loyal house companions these days.

Like typical Aquarians, cocker spaniels love social gatherings and adore all of their friends equally. "The more the merrier!" is this happy tail wagger's motto. "Kids and other pets are welcome, too!" Life is too short to spend it alone; friends are people and animals you choose to be around. Why not have a lot of them? Who would you share all of those zany ideas with? We're all cool, why don't we all hang out? The cocker spaniels live for their buddies and want them to love each other, too.

REAL-LIFE EXAMPLES OF COCKER SPANIEL/AQUARIUS TRAITS

- Anisse, Lola, and Shiraz are inseparable and love lounging in cafes and meeting new friends all over the world with their parents. How do you think we met them? Just casually chilling at one of New York's hippest restaurants, of course. They wagged their tails at us, and it was love at first sight.
- These characters have already charmed their way into Italian *Vogue*, *Cosmopolitan*, and of course, *Dog Stars*; just wait till they get an offer for a doggie TV show without even trying—or even wanting one! People just love them!

DOG STAR

Pisces

(February 19 – March 20)

THE PISCES DOG

ELEMENT: Water

MODALITY: Mutable

RULERSHIP: Neptune

SYMBOL: Fish

MOST COMPATIBLE WITH: Cancer, Scorpio, Taurus, and Capricorn

WHAT A PISCES DOG DAYDREAMS ABOUT: nirvana; sleepathons; trips to the ocean; saving humanity

KEYWORDS: dreamy, fantasy, shy, empathic, compassion, imaginative, messy, creative, spiritual, great dancer

THE PISCES DOG STAR'S PERSONALITY

))(The Pisces dog loves to escape reality.

))(The Pisces dog could sleep for three days straight.

))(The Pisces dog lives in his own fairy tale world.

))(The Pisces dog thrives on chaos.

))(The Pisces dog is here to give unconditional love and compassion.

))(The Pisces dog is a psychic sponge and will absorb all the energy in the home.

))(The Pisces dog takes on all of your mannerisms.

))(The Pisces dog empathizes with everyone.

))(The Pisces dog wants to merge with everyone and everything. All is one.

STAR SIGN CHARACTERISTICS

MERRILY, MERRILY, MERRILY, MERRILY . . .

Life is a dream, or at least an eternal snooze when it comes to your Pisces pup. Don't count on this doggie to be your alarm clock. She'd prefer it if you hit the snooze button a few zillion times. This precocious pup can teach you the deepest spiritual lessons without uttering a word ("He who knows, does not speak. He who speaks, does not know," Lao-tzu). If you want to witness unconditional love

✳

170

and empathy in action, observe the saintly behaviors of your divine canine friend. The chilled-out Piscean Dog Star will show you what it truly means to relax and let your mind drift downstream.

To Be a Dog or Not to Be, That Is the Question . . .

The Pisces doggie is as poetic as Shakespeare: Like Will, she knows that life is but a stage where grown-ups simply don strange costumes and act like a bunch of egotistical lunatics trying to outdo one another. The innocent Pisces Dog Star has no interest in competition or worldly stresses. She is the least ambitious of the Dog Stars. The Pisces pup is here to remind you not to fall prey to the snares of illusion and delusion. She only wants to love and be loved in return and she hopes the same for you, dummy. Consider this four-legged furry friend your guru and wake up to the deep teachings of unconditional love and forgiveness. If that's too Chopra for you, at least get a grip and stop taking this life so seriously. Dream or die.

Sleeping Beauty

Sure, all dogs spend a good portion of their lives catching zzz's but this dog treats sleep like a religion. Unlike most dogs that jump up in ecstasy should you merely spell the *w* word—as in *w-a-l-k*—the Pisces will burrow herself in farther under the covers, hoping you won't dare interrupt her dreamtime. Dreaming is what she does best. Should you catch your little Pisces Dog Star dreaming of deep-sea diving as strange gurgling, water-bubble sounds abound in the midst of her dreamtime, just chalk it up to her vivid imagination. Lord only knows where she might have traveled while all snuggled up in her favorite doggie bed. She might even astral travel in her sleep, which means she can go spy on your aunt June's dog or connect with other Dog Stars across the continent. She has even been known to do some long-distance healing on people in crisis or trauma. This mystical doggie is as deep as the ocean.

TELEPADOG

Oh, and we should probably mention that the Pisces Dog Star is a psychic sponge if not totally telepathic. She totally picks up the vibes in the household and people. If you need someone to sniff out whether your latest date is trustworthy or a good character, watch your psychic pup in action. She'll have ways of letting you know if the new stranger in the home is to be trusted or sent to the curb. Oh, and definitely watch what you think. She does. She can read your mind and moods and contact the deceased like her name was Sylvia Browne. If she seems a bit skittish or paranoid, it's just her hypersensitivity. Handle this darling with the utmost care; the Pisces dog is a truly mystical being. The more you meditate and sleep late, the happier your little swami will be. She is ultrasensitive to the surrounding atmosphere so be sure to give your beloved Pisces pooch sweet music, beautiful candles, and a running fountain if you don't live near the ocean (she adores the sound of water). You'll kill her with the mundane and the blasé.

FURRY SAVIOR

The Pisces Dog Star believes she is here to save you and the rest of the unenlightened dodo heads out there. She is plugged into the ethereal realms, where all the doggie angels and guides hang out. She will give you endless supplies of spiritual nourishment just by her own highly evolved displays of patience, forgiveness, and understanding. Should you see your little Jesus doggie bearing a cross, quickly trade it for a Milk-Bone dog biscuit to prevent any serious displays of martyrdom. But seriously, this doggie would do anything to make your life easier and your soul happier. She lives to serve and sacrifice for those she loves. In fact, she loves you so completely that she may not know where she ends and you begin.

IF THE PISCES DOG COULD TALK

Boy, could I use a scotch on the rocks right about now.

Pull those shades back down. I'm light sensitive.

Your bad mood is rubbing off on me—cheer up, wouldya?!

Do we have to go out? I'm so drained.

Could you get your hands on some puppy uppers?

Life can be so brutal sometimes.

You call it sleeping? I call it connecting with the divine.

Please keep your energy-sucking relatives away from me;

it takes me hours to recover.

Spare me the reality checks, buster. I'll take the dream over reality any day.

I don't know where I've been the last couple of weeks.

Don't wake me . . . I'm about to reach Nirvana.

WHAT A PISCES DOG WANTS IN AN OWNER

SOMEWHERE, A PLACE FOR US

I want my soul mate! Aren't there any gentle souls left in this cold, hard world? If you're a crazy type-A personality and/or up at the crack of dawn, puhleeez, pretty please: Don't pick me. You'll ruin my idea of a fantasy world in .00003 seconds. Dearly beloved, I need my beauty rest and then some more. You see, I have much more to process than the average dog because I see and feel everything as if it were happening to me. Sleep is my medicine, my cure, my salvation. If this is going to work between us, please do your best to understand my undying quest to uncover the subtle complexities of my unconscious. I need someone who will appreciate how spiritual sleeping can be. Let's analyze my dreams together and then paint and do some dance therapy. I could listen to sweet music 24/7, that, and movie marathons—any excuse to curl up and do nothing but turn my doggie thoughts off and take off to another reality. I'm a dreamer by nature and prefer someone who will let me keep my illusions, and make this a heaven on earth complete with aromatherapy balm for my fur, endless petting, and pet pampering plus.

CARE OF THE SOUL

I need a guide (never say *master*) who lives according to the dictates of their soul. If that sounds too deep, you are probably not the one for me. I am super-sensitive and need you to appreciate how vulnerable this world makes me feel. I prefer to live away from toxic places with too many people or too much noise. I'd be psyched if it could be just the two of us. I don't do well with large groups of people or families because I totally absorb the energy and vibes in the room—for real, I do.

I'd be happy to live in a small cottage near the ocean or in a fabulous hipster pad with glamour galore. It's all about the glamour; I have a particular love for Lucite and Phillipe Starck furniture. If you happen to be the pragmatic type, you might drive me to drink. I need an ideal atmosphere that encourages my mind to wander to blissful and fantastic places. The more Salvador Dali the better.

CHAOS IS THE HIGHEST LEVEL OF ORGANIZATION

I prefer the messy variety when it comes to owners. You see, it makes more sense to me to mess up my dog bed and all your stuff, too, while I'm at it. I can find my bones and toys better in a mess than when everything is too neat and tidy. I love an owner who functions well in chaos. The less structured you are, the better. Discipline makes me suddenly develop an extreme case of narcolepsy. I believe in going with the flow and letting things evolve of their own accord. As one of my favorite spiritual dogs once told me, "Let the thing announce itself," rather than push the issue. Rigidity makes me extremely paranoid, I'll have you know. I'm fine with random walks and extra naps. But throw me into some kind of doggie boot camp and I'm likely to have a doggie breakdown. I'm fragile so I need someone who will handle me with the utmost care.

HOW TO EARN BROWNIE POINTS
FROM A PISCES DOGGIE

Princess pillows	20 pts
Lavender baths	20 pts

Dreamy and cozy home	20 pts
Homemade treats	20 pts
Two short walks a day, max	20 pts
	100 pts

COMPATIBILITY GUIDE

Most compatible with: Cancer, Scorpio, Taurus, Capricorn

A PISCES DOG WITH AN ARIES OWNER

Ouch. This combo could be painful for the sensitive Pisces pooch if the Aries human doesn't keep her fiery impulses in check. The Pisces has a delicate soul and the Aries will have to learn to behave accordingly. The forever-forgiving Pisces pup will overlook any outbursts or tantrums and return unconditional love and sweetness. The Aries human can teach this sleepy pooch how to rev up the doggie gusto for a marathon of speed fetch until both finally pass out from exhaustion. Yeah, right—don't think so.

A PISCES DOG WITH A TAURUS OWNER

This combination is effortless, enviable, if not a doggone MGM musical in the making. These two actually like to sing mushy songs together. Their dog-human chemistry is like "buttah, darling." With the Taurus human's patience and gentle nature mixed with the serenity of the Pisces angelic dog, nothing could disturb their peace and bliss. A Pisces dog loves drinking multiple beverages and a Taurus Bull loves big pig helpings; life is like one big food festival 365 days a year.

A Pisces Dog with a Gemini Owner

Major issue: You bring out the ADD tendencies in each other, so you'll never know which end is up. The Pisces pup can be a bit of a space cadet and a Gemini human a bit of a brilliant ditz. But the Pisces will love it when the Gemini human tells long-winded bedtime stories full of fantastical characters and dreamy endings. Likewise, the Gemini human is fascinated by the chameleonlike tendencies of the Pisces pup with strange moods and doggie mannerisms depending on where they've been that day. The Gemini human has better mysteries to solve than this celestial, bordering on alien, canine.

A Pisces Dog with a Cancer Owner

These two water-loving creatures will need a second home by the ocean or a yacht, or just their own private Idaho to recover from daily interactions with energy-sucking humans. But together they shelter each other from the hard edges in life. They are both moody and often compete for victim status. The Pisces yelps wolf and the Cancer never lets go of the past. Anything to get some extra TLC; but who will really take care of who? There may be some serious role confusion with this match because both insist on being the baby. Just give these two softies a good acupuncturist and some Chinese herbs and life is a walk in the park once more.

A PISCES DOG WITH A LEO OWNER

The Pisces pup likes to remain incognito, whereas the Leo human prefers to strut her pride and joy around like Hollywood royalty. But in the end, it's a match because the Pisces will always worship at the altar of her Leo human. While the Leo is out networking, the Pisces dog is contacting the right angels in order to hook the Leo up with the next big gig. They both need to live a glamorous life and would never be caught without their makeup and hair done! The only difference is that the Leo has to convince the Pisces to wake up from their marathon snooze in time to make the next big happening.

A PISCES DOG WITH A VIRGO OWNER

With Virgo and Pisces, it's the two of them against the rest of the world. Both are hermits at heart who'd rather shelter themselves from crowds and worldliness in general. Gentle souls who need to be of service, this match will feel like a calling from above. The only pitfall: The Pisces doggie's messy ways could send the Virgo into a major OCD freak-out. The Pisces dog could easily enter a state of hypertension as she'll absorb every fear and worry the Virgo human has. As long as the Virgo trains his spacey little dog how to eat out of his dish without spilling food everywhere, their shared hermitage could lead them both to nirvana when they're hiding out together.

A PISCES DOG WITH A LIBRA OWNER

Beautiful ambiance is the key to this dog's and human's well-being. Neither can stomach ugliness, so the household will be a model for harmony and home design.

The Libra will lavish her Pisces dog with every goody imaginable, especially treats. Since the Libra rarely falls into extreme mood swings, the Pisces doggie's strong sensitivity won't be in danger of becoming overwhelmed. This is an easy, breezy combo of sweetness and light. Everyone else may get a cavity just looking at the two of you walking down the street together. Aww.

A PISCES DOG WITH A SCORPIO OWNER

At last, the Scorpio human has found a soul mate in doggie form. When their eyes first meet there's instant recognition that these two have known each other many lifetimes. The Pisces dog forgives the Scorpio human's stings and shortcomings; the Scorpio human lets the Pisces escape into doggie fantasy whenever she so desires. They both love a dark, candlelit household. And since they're both nocturnal creatures, they love watching late-night television together. This combo constitutes the kind of serious empathy and bond that actually will last for an eternity.

A PISCES DOG WITH A SAGITTARIUS OWNER

The boppy Sag human might feel more than a wee bit watered down by the sensitive, sleepaholic Pisces pooch. Thin-skinned Pisces poochie might feel overwhelmed by the Sag human's bluntness and nonstop energy. The Pisces dog dreams of faraway places but never actually goes anywhere except her doggy bed and around the block for walks when she absolutely can't hold it anymore; the Sag will want to change all that. But with early and proper training, the reluctant Pisces dreaming doggie might learn to appreciate the exercise and excitement that the screwball Sag human can provide—*not!*

✳

A PISCES DOG WITH A CAPRICORN OWNER

A soothing Pisces pooch could be just what the doctor ordered for the overachieving Capricorn. This pup will teach the Cap how to relax. Spend now, worry later, that's the Pisces pup's mantra. "Life is too short to be so conservative," says Pisces pooch. The Capricorn human might learn to work less and sleep and dream a little more. In turn, the Pisces doggie will learn the value of money from the Capricorn—sometimes it pays to be realistic, especially when it comes to those expensive doggie treats.

A PISCES DOG WITH AN AQUARIUS OWNER

These kids live in the way-off future together. They're so far ahead of the rest of the schmo's out there. Together these two were built to stir up the status quo and raise a little Cain. The Pisces pup loves mischief and can be as quirky and spontaneous as the wacky Aquarius. Ever in search of a good friend (a real friend, not just an acquaintance) the Pisces doggie will have the Aquarius human hooked with his sweetie-pie soulfulness and commitment to dreaming big dreams. It may sound like pie in the sky to other mere mortals, but this dream team can visualize and manifest big things, like vacations in Bhutan and purple Corvettes.

A PISCES DOG WITH A PISCES OWNER

This pair is divinity incarnate: one-half dog, one-half human equals total enlightenment. Between endless hours of meditation and catching some zzz's, they'll find time for the movies and trips to the ballet. But when reality or the bill collector calls, at least one of them has to answer the phone. Avoidance tactics like email or text messaging don't count. As long as the Pisces human remembers to wake them both up for an occasional walk, no one will even raise an eye at the lifestyle of eternal sleepfests and movie marathons.

TYPICAL PISCES BREEDS

Pug, Collie, and Newfoundland

STAR SIGHTING: ROXY—PUG

Just look at those watery, dreamy, and sensitive eyes! Can any dog be more Piscean than a pug? Gentle, sweet, affectionate, loving, charming, loyal, friendly, playful, independent, and sleepy, this little character is best for someone who is in need of constant therapy or on a spiritual quest. In fact, the Pug's ancestors were once companions of Buddhist priests—a Pisces's dream!!

A pug is a heavenly house dog: She doesn't require much space as long as you give her a comfortable bed, good food, and a lot of love and affection. This little friend from la-la land is a perfect lap dog/couch potato if you're not on the active side. Some pugs are more energetic than others, of course. A short walk to the local deli would be plenty of exercise, though. Joggers need not apply.

REAL-LIFE EXAMPLES OF PUG/PISCES TRAITS

- Roxy would much rather curl up in her comfy, fuzzy little bed at home than go for walks.
- Roxy meditates daily to her purple bear guru.
- Roxy is a practicing pet-therapist.

Conclusion

NOW THAT YOU'VE gotten the inside scoop to your doggie's true inner Star nature, we hope that these insights will provide you with an even deeper bond based on a new appreciation for the complexities of the canine personality. Even if you don't believe dogs are people, too (but we highly doubt that)—you have to now admit they are all stars in their own right. Whether they steal your heart or your bank account, your Dog Star has descended from the celestial beings to guide, protect, and offer eternal unconditionally loving companionship for life. Your Dog Star will even watch over you when they return back to the stars. They are guardian angels while on earth and forever after.

References

American Kennel Club's Web site: http://www.akc.org

Bailey, Gwen. *Choosing the Right Dog for You.* New York: Barnes & Noble Books, 2004.

Dog Breed Info Center: www.dogbreedinfo.com

Dog Owner's Guide: www.canismajor.com

Fogle, Bruce, D.V.M. *The New Encyclopedia of the Dog.* New York: Dorling Kindersley, 2000.

Index

Numbers in *italics* are illustrations.